Contents

F   Foreword by Professor Dermot Mc Aleese

1.   Employment and Unemployment in Ireland during the 1980s   1

2.   What People Earn in Ireland   11

3.   Pay versus Prices   18

4.   The Weighty Burden of Personal Tax in the 1980s   27

5.   The Tax Wedge   37

6.   The Social Welfare Safety Net   54

7.   The Low-Paid   68

8.   Searching for Lower Taxes Abroad   80

9.   Making Sense of the Labour Market   88

10.   The Way Ahead   96

BUSINESS AND ECONOMICS RESEARCH SERIES

General Editor: Professor Dermot McAleese (Trinity College, Dublin)

Competition and Industry
Ireland's Changing Demographic Structure
Small Firm Competitiveness and Performance
Privatisation: Issues of Principle and Implementation in Ireland

Forthcoming:

Overseas Industry in Ireland
Transport Policy in Ireland in the 1990s

MAKING THE IRISH LABOUR MARKET WORK

Paul Tansey

Gill and Macmillan

Published in Ireland by
Gill and Macmillan Ltd
Goldenbridge
Dublin 8

with associated companies in
Auckland, Delhi, Gaborone, Hamburg, Harare,
Hong Kong, Johannesburg, Kuala Lumpur, Lagos, London,
Manzini, Melbourne, Mexico City, Nairobi,
New York, Singapore, Tokyo

Designed by The Unlimited Design Company, Dublin

Print origination by Seton Music Graphics, Bantry, Co. Cork

Printed by Colour Books Ltd, Dublin

British Library Cataloguing in Publication Data
Tansey, Paul
Making the Irish labour market work.
— (Business and economics research series)
I. Title II. Series
331.1309417

ISBN 0-7171-1919-X

FOREWORD

Professor Dermot McAleese

Paul Tansey has been described as the thinking person's economic jounalist. Readers of this monograph will understand why. Those familiar with his past writings in the *Irish Times* and his current contributions to the *Sunday Tribune* will happily recognise the attention to statistical detail, the careful ordering of argument, the scrupulous demarcation between fact and inference, and the ability to communicate clearly without either oversimplification or talking-down. In discussing the Irish labour market he writes with authority; he is well acquainted with the data, with the literature, and with the complex nature of the problems of job creation and unemployment in the Irish economy.

The book is not a polemic. Instead it offers a clinical assessment of what has gone wrong and how matters can be improved. Tansey's thesis adds up to an indictment of economic policy as it has affected the labour market, all the more damning for being dispassionate.

It would be wrong for me to try to summarise the arguments of the book; and the author does this expertly in the final two chapters. Certain themes are, however, worth emphasising.

First, the growth in taxation by stealth is documented. This happened through non-indexation of tax allowances and tax bands, and the introduction of new taxes in the guise of contributions to health, training, and social insurance. The result: next to Iceland, Ireland has the highest standard income tax rate in the OECD; and the numbers paying higher than the standard tax rate have risen dramatically.

Second, this increase in taxation created a wedge between cost of labour to the employer and net income of the employee. The cost to employers of providing the average single employee a £1 increase in net income rose from £1.82 in 1980/81 to £2.55 in 1987/88. Firms paying above the average face even greater costs. The result: *no* other OECD country has a tax system as biased against the use of labour as the Irish.

Third, social welfare payments have been increased and extended without reference to the tax system. (Tansey notes in passing that the number of people claiming social welfare benefits stands at 715,540, while the total number of beneficiaries including children has reached 1.3 million. This reflects not the extent of poverty but the grossly over-extended reach of social welfare schemes.) The unintended side-effect of this rise in entitlements has been a hefty increase in replacement ratios. Families with one spouse unemployed, single people and above all the low-paid and the long-term unemployed have been particularly affected. The analysis of the position of the low-paid, to which a special chapter is devoted, merits careful study. The result: returning to work has been made steadily less attractive financially for those groups most in need of integration into the labour market.

These three themes are developed skilfully in the book, with full attention to the nuances, exceptions, and special cases. They illustrate how economic policy has for most of the past two decades adversely affected the labour market, despite the chronic need for more jobs. Numbers entering the active age-group grew just as they were predicted to grow. To keep them at work in Ireland required policies that would have made labour more attractive to hire. Economists like Paul Tansey who tried to call a halt were, alas, ignored.

The direction of policy has improved somewhat in recent years. The role of better management of the economy is given its due:

While the strength of demand conditions abroad and the revival of demand at home played the principal part in improving labour market conditions in the final years of the decade, the impact of specific measures geared towards making the labour market work more effectively cannot be ignored, and should not be neglected (p. 89).

These measures include the reduction in tax rates, widening of the tax bands, and special measures to help the low-paid. Tansey argues that policy must continue firmly in this direction. His case is compelling: lower taxes generally, special attention to employment traps for the low-income groups, and parallel development if not full integration of the tax and welfare systems. He does not claim that such measures will solve Ireland's unemployment problem; but, pursued vigorously, they would certainly bring about a significant improvement.

'Pursued vigorously' is the operative phrase. By mid-1991 it appears that the progress made has been too slow to make a real indent in the problems posed for the Irish labour market by a UK economy hit by a severe recession. Indeed, as Paul Tansey himself (and others, such as Dr Seán Barrett of Trinity College) has pointed out elsewhere, the Government's failure to tackle the problem of public sector pay and its slackening control of public expenditure mark a worsening in the parameters of the Irish labour market.

This book does not claim to provide a fully comprehensive account of the labour market. Thus the role of trade unions and the effects of labour legislation on the labour market are not analysed. Regulations on unfair dismissals, equal pay, part-time work and conditions of work also impact on the demand/supply equation. Yet the dynamics of their introduction seemed to operate quite independently of the level of unemployment or the need for more jobs in Ireland. Generally the practice has been to follow British or EC legislation when it 'favours' the workers—meaning by that of course the fortunate subset of the labour force who happen to have jobs and are able to retain them. In this way Ireland has acquired a labour market regime, in terms of protection of worker rights and trade union privileges, that stands comparison with the best in Europe. Wonderful for the lucky ones with jobs! But their benefit is at the cost of the outsiders: those unable to find work, those in the informal sector, and Irish emigrants who must work in less benign and less well-protected labour markets.

The Irish labour market has, as Paul Tansey says, performed abysmally in the 1980s. It need not have been so. Other countries, ranging from Portugal to the United States, have achieved notable success in job generation and lower unemployment. This book provides an excellent analysis of what has gone wrong in Ireland and how we could do better.

EMPLOYMENT AND UNEMPLOYMENT IN IRELAND DURING THE 1980s

For the Irish economy, the 1980s were a disappointment. For much of the decade the economy languished in a torpor, seemingly unable or unwilling to extract itself from the difficulties that beset it. Most of the problems in the economic domain traced their origins to a single source. For much of the 1980s Ireland suffered a painfully slow rate of economic expansion; economic growth at home was deficient in both quantity and quality. The symptoms of slow growth manifested themselves in many ugly forms. Unemployment was persistently high. Net emigration re-emerged on a mass scale from the middle of the decade. Living standards stood still for the first half of the 1980s. And all the while the state was falling ever deeper into debt, adding to the burdens imposed on future generations of taxpayers.

It was not until the final years of the decade that robust rates of growth returned. The gains in employment and living standards, in reduced taxes and booming investment registered in the final years of the 1980s served only to underline the opportunities that had been lost in earlier years. Yet the growth revival from 1987 onwards planted the seeds of a new approach to running the economy. The years of economic stagnation had been associated with rising rates of Government spending, accompanied by a sharp and continuous increase in the burden of taxes. Despite the additional tax impositions, annual current budget deficits widened, prompting a recourse to ever more extensive Government borrowing. Despite the financial impetus provided by the Government, the economy had refused to grow for much of the 1980s.

The 'new departure' of the final years of the decade consisted of reversing completely the approach of previous years. Government spending—current and capital—was cut back severely from 1987. From 1988 onwards, continuous reductions were effected in income taxes. The economy boomed and bloomed in response, providing the additional revenue buoyancy that caused Government borrowing to fall sharply.

The dualism of Irish economic experience during the 1980s—virtual stagnation until 1987 and a robust economic revival thereafter—teaches two clear lessons. First, the state through its spending, no matter how extensive, cannot make the economy a success. Second, lower taxes can assist in improving economic performance. The principal features of economic performance during the 1980s are shown in table 1. As can be seen, economic progress in the decade's final years far surpassed performance in the early 1980s.

Table 1

Economic growth, living standards and employment in Ireland, 1980–89

Year	Real GDP index	Real GNP index	Real consumer spending index	Total at work (000, April)	Real GNP per capita index
(indices are based on 1980 = 100)					
1980	100	100	100	1,156	100
1981	103.3	102.6	101.7	1,146	101.4
1982	105.7	101.9	94.6	1,146	99.7
1983	105.5	100.3	95.4	1,124	97.3
1984	110.1	102.6	97.3	1,103	99.0
1985	112.9	103.6	100.7	1,079	99.7
1986	112.4	102.4	102.7	1,081	·98.3
1987	117.3	107.5	105.0	1,080	103.1
1988	121.9	109.0	107.6	1,091	104.8
1989	129.1	114.5	113.1	1,090	110.9
Change 1980–89	29.1%	14.5%	13.1%	–5.7%	10.9%

Sources: The indices for real GDP, real GNP and real aggregate personal consumer spending are calculated from data in the *National Income and Expenditure* tables for the years 1986–89, published by the Central Statistics Office. The totals at work relate to April of each year and are derived from the revised *Labour Force Survey* for the years shown. The index for per capita GNP is calculated by applying the annual estimates of population in the *Economic Review and Outlook, 1990*, table 14, to the index of real GNP.

At first sight, the harvest of economic growth reaped during the 1980s does not appear too niggardly. Between 1980 and 1989 real gross domestic product increased by more than 29 per cent in aggregate terms. While Ireland was a late entrant to the European economic recovery of the 1980s, the pace of Irish economic growth accelerated sharply from 1987 onwards.

However, the dynamic effects of this seemingly rapid growth in real GDP were greatly diluted by large and continuous outflows of net factor income over the course of the decade. These net outflows of income from Ireland to the rest of the world reflected the operation of two quite different sets of economic forces. Firstly, a substantial part of the outflow mirrored the rising cost of servicing Ireland's accumulated stock of foreign debt. External indebtedness rose from 24.5 per cent of gross national product in 1980 to 43.7 per cent in 1989. The rising burden of foreign debt—and the very high real interest that obtained for most of the decade—required that an increasing proportion of each year's income be diverted from the domestic economy to foreign lenders in order to service outstanding debts. Secondly, repatriation of profits, dividends, royalties and interest by transnational companies operating in Ireland increased as the decade progressed. It was the very success of these companies' exports from Irish production facilities that provided the principal stimulus to GDP growth for most of the decade; yet the apparent impetus they imparted to domestic economic growth through export expansion was greatly weakened by the subsequent repatriation of income earned in Ireland.

Nor was it only foreign transnational corporations that reinvested their Irish earnings abroad during the 1980s. Faced with a stagnant domestic economy, many leading Irish publicly quoted companies went abroad in search of additional profits during the 1980s: the Jefferson Smurfit Group, Allied Irish Banks, Bank of Ireland, Cement-Roadstone Holdings, Waterford Glass and James Crean PLC all sought expansion through foreign acquisitions during the decade. The combined operation of these two forces—the rising cost of servicing a growing stock of foreign debt, and the outflow of corporate earnings from the domestic economy—caused the net factor income outflow to drive a large wedge between the growth in real GDP and real GNP as the 1980s unfolded.

The divergence between real GDP growth and real GNP growth during the 1980s is illustrated in table 1. As can be seen, real GNP increased only half as fast as real GDP during the decade. While GDP rose by over 29 per cent between 1980 and 1989, there was virtually no growth in real GNP between 1980 and 1986; and over the decade as a whole, real GNP increased by just 14.5 per cent. Per head of population, real GNP increased at an even slower pace over the decade, because of population growth. The state's estimated population in April 1980 was 3.401 million; by the time of the 1986 census it had risen to 3.541 million, an increase of 140,000 or 4.1 per cent on its estimated level in 1980. Over this period aggregate GNP in real terms increased by less than 2.5 per cent. Thus by 1986, GNP per capita was *lower* than it had been in 1980. It was only the strength of the economic revival from 1987 onwards, together with the decline in absolute population after that year, that allowed GNP per capita to show the 10.9 per cent increase recorded for the decade as a whole.

Real GNP—rather than real GDP—represents the resources retained in the domestic economy to finance investment, the creation of jobs, and improvements in living standards. As can be seen from table 1, the volume of aggregate personal consumer expenditure was no higher in 1985 than in 1980, so that all the gains in living standards were recorded in the second half of the decade. For the 1980s as a whole, real consumer spending rose by 13.1 per cent, closely in step with the overall rise in real GNP.

While economic growth was poor during the 1980s, with real GNP growth averaging only 1.5 per cent a year, the employment performance was even worse. Between April 1980 and April 1989 the total number at work declined by 66,000 or 5.7 per cent. The preliminary results of the 1990 labour force survey indicate that employment increased by 30,000 in the year to April 1990. Even allowing for this very substantial increase in employment over that year, the total number at work, at 1.120 million by April 1990, was still 36,000 or 3.1 per cent below the level of a decade earlier.

Even in those productive sectors of the economy that experienced significant growth during the 1980s, the employment performance was disappointing. Thus, between 1980 and 1989, while the volume of production in manufacturing industry increased by 90 per cent, the number employed in manufacturing fell by more than 40,000 or almost 18 per cent. Gross agricultural product— farm outputs less inputs—increased by 20 per cent between 1980 and 1989; yet the number of people engaged in agriculture declined by 22 per cent over the same period. (Each of these trends is illustrated in table 2.) If demand conditions in the economy were relatively weak for most of the 1980s, then the demand for labour was weakest of all.

On the supply side of the labour market, the very rapid increase in population during the 1970s (much of it caused by significant net immigration) established the conditions for large annual additions to the labour force during the 1980s. While the size of the labour force did increase significantly in the early years of the 1980s, this process stopped abruptly after 1983; by

Table 2				
Changes in output and employment in manufacturing and agriculture, 1980–89				
Year	Index of manufacturing output (1980 = 100)	Manufacturing employment (000)	Index of gross farm product (1980 = 100)	Agricultural employment (000)
1980	100	227.2	100	209
1981	106.0	222.5	95.0	196
1982	104.9	215.3	106.6	193
1983	113.7	202.5	108.4	189
1984	125.0	195.6	125.4	181
1985	130.6	186.9	121.2	171
1986	134.4	184.2	112.0	168
1987	149.8	182.1	118.8	164
1988	168.6	182.4	121.6	166
1989	190.0	186.6	120.2	163
Change 1980–89	90.0%	−17.9%	20.2%	−22.0%

Sources: The volume of output in manufacturing industry is computed by the Central Statistics Office. Manufacturing employment data is collected by the CSO in its *Quarterly Industrial Inquiry*. Gross farm product represents gross agricultural output less inputs of materials and services. The latest figures are extracted from the *Economic Review and Outlook, 1990*, Table 11. The trend in agricultural employment is as shown in the CSO's annual Labour Force Surveys.

April 1990 the labour force was smaller than it had been seven years earlier.

When the recession induced by the oil crisis of 1979–80 hit the economy, the initial shock to employment was absorbed primarily by a rise in the level of unemployment. Between April 1980 and April 1983 unemployment doubled, from 91,000 to 183,000. As can be seen from the data in table 3, over these years roughly two-thirds of the increase in unemployment was accounted for by the growth in the labour force, one-third by the contraction in employment.

Table 3

Profile of the Irish labour market, 1980–90 (000)

All figures relate to April of the year concerned

Year	Total at work	Unemploy-ment	Labour force	Net emigration*	Population
1990	1,120	183	1,303	–31	3,503
1989	1,090	202	1,292	–46	3,515
1988	1,091	219	1,310	–32	3,538
1987	1,080	232	1,312	–27	3,543
1986	1,081	227	1,308	–28	3,541
1985	1,079	226	1,305	–20	3,540
1984	1,103	204	1,307	–9	3,529
1983	1,124	183	1,307	–14	3,504
1982	1,146	147	1,293	–1	3,480
1981	1,146	126	1,272	2	3,443
1980	1,156	91	1,247	–8	3,401

*The net emigration figures represent the change since April of the preceding year
Sources: The Labour Force Surveys, taken every two years between 1975 and 1983 and annually thereafter, provide the data shown here for the totals at work, unemployment, and the labour force. The Central Statistics Office published preliminary estimates for the 1990 Labour Force Survey in October 1990. The figures for 1980 and 1982 are CSO estimates. Note that surveyed unemployment differs from registered unemployment. Estimates for net migration are published annually by the CSO, as are between-census estimates of population. The data for the year to April 1990 was published in the CSO's *Economic Series*, August 1990. The population figures for 1981 and 1986 are census figures.

While the initial impact of the recession on the labour market manifested itself in sharply increased unemployment, as it became apparent that domestic employment opportunities were not going to improve, net emigration began once again, and at increasingly rapid rates as the decade advanced. In the eight years from April 1982 to April 1990 net emigration reached 207,000. Even as economic conditions improved in the final years of the decade, there was little abatement in the net annual emigration rate.

In the year to April 1990, a year in which the preliminary results of the 1990 labour force survey found that 30,000 jobs had been added to the work force, net emigration still reached 31,000. This massive and sustained outflow of Irish people from their country has caused profound changes in the profile of the labour market. First, continuous emigration has halted the expansion of the labour force: as noted earlier, the domestic labour force was smaller in April 1990 than it was seven years earlier. Second, high levels of net emigration each year have acted as a brake on the rise in unemployment. On the basis of the labour force survey, unemployment peaked at 232,000 in April 1987. However, the constant attrition of emigration meant that by 1989 unemployment had fallen back to its 1984 level. The combination of rapid employment growth and a further large net outflow of emigrants in the year to April 1990 caused unemployment at that date to return to its 1983 level of 183,000. Third, the sheer scale of net emigration over a sustained period, coupled with a fall in the birth rate and thus the natural rate of population growth, has induced a decline in population. In 1987 the population reached a recent peak at 3.543 million; in the ensuing three years the number declined by 40,000, to 3,503 million. (These trends can be inspected in detail in table 3.)

The economy thus experienced failure on two fronts during the 1980s. First, the quantity of economic growth generated and retained in the economy—real GNP growth—was too low. Second, the quality of growth, in terms of the employment dividends it yielded, was poor for most of the decade.

The extent of these failures can be gauged by comparing Ireland's economic record against those of other industrial countries over much of the last decade. Such a comparison, spanning the years 1979 to 1987, is presented in table 4, using annual average rates of employment and economic growth and annual average unemployment rates as performance indicators. The table encapsulates the performance of each of the twenty-

Table 4

Economic growth, employment expansion and unemployment rates in the OECD, 1979–87

Countries are ranked by the real average annual growth rates achieved. Relative performance on other indicators is shown in parentheses.

Rank	Country	Real GDP/ GNP growth rate (%)	Annual average growth in jobs (%)	Average unemployment rate (%)
1	Turkey	4.6	2.0 (2)	11.2 (22)
2	Japan	3.9	0.9 (12)	2.5 (6)
3	Iceland	3.8	3.2 (1)	0.7 (2)
4	Norway	3.6	1.4 (6)	2.4 (5)
5	Finland	3.2	0.9 (12)	5.2 (9)
6	Australia	3.0	1.9 (3)	7.6 (13)
7	Canada	2.9	1.7 (4)	9.5 (18)
8	Luxembourg	2.6	1.0 (9)	1.3 (3)
9	United States	2.4	1.6 (5)	7.5 (12)
10	Portugal	2.3	1.1 (7)	8.0 (14)
11	Italy	2.2	0.3 (17)	9.6 (20)
12	Spain	2.1	−0.8 (24)	16.9 (24)
13	Britain	2.0	−0.1 (20)	9.6 (20)
14	Switzerland	2.0	0.6 (14)	0.6 (1)
15	Sweden	2.0	0.5 (15)	2.2 (4)
16	Denmark	2.0	0.8 (13)	8.6 (17)
17	New Zealand	2.0	0.9 (12)	3.7 (8)
18	France	1.7	−0.2 (21)	8.6 (17)
19	Austria	1.6	0.2 (18)	2.9 (7)
20	Belgium	1.5	−0.3 (22)	11.0 (21)
21	Germany (Federal Republic)	1.4	0.4 (16)	5.3 (10)
22	IRELAND	1.3	−0.6 (23)	13.1 (23)
23	Netherlands	1.2	−0.1 (20)	8.1 (15)
24	Greece	1.2	1.0 (9)	5.9
	EC average	1.8	0.1	9.1
	OECD average	2.5	0.9	7.3

Source: OECD *Employment Outlook*, Paris, July 1990 (calculated from tables 1.A.1 to 1.A.3).

four member-states of the Organisation for Economic Co-operation and Development on each of the selected indicators. Ireland's comparative performance can be summarised thus:

—Of the twenty-four countries surveyed, Ireland ranked twenty-second in terms of the expansiveness of its growth rate. In the years 1979 to 1987 Ireland managed an average growth rate of 1.3 per cent a year; over the same period, economic growth averaged 1.8 per cent a year in the European Community and 2.5 per cent a year in the OECD as a whole.

—Ireland ranked twenty-third in terms of its ability to create and retain employment. In the years 1979 to 1987, total employment in Ireland declined by 0.6 per cent a year on average; over the same period the EC managed to achieve marginal employment gains each year, while in the industrial world as a whole, employment expanded by almost 1 per cent a year on average.

—Ireland ranked twenty-third in terms of its ability to contain unemployment. Through the years 1979 to 1987 unemployment as a percentage of the labour force averaged 13.1 per cent; Ireland's unemployment rate was thus almost half as high again as the EC average over these years and almost twice the average OECD rate of 7.1 per cent.

Thus, of the twenty-four industrial countries that comprise the OECD, only Spain had a worse record on employment creation and unemployment rates than Ireland; while in the growth league, only the Netherlands and Greece put in a weaker performance.

The data in table 4 suggests that in most cases there is quite a strong association between the pace of economic growth and the extent of additions to employment. Countries recording above average rates of economic growth tend to generate significant employment gains. In contrast, countries experiencing below average growth tend to have experienced a contraction in employment.

X The detailed reasons for Ireland's poor record on economic growth over the past decade lie beyond the scope of the present study. However, it is worth noting that the revival of economic growth in recent years has been accompanied by net additions to the numbers at work. Attention is directed in this book to examining policies that would strengthen the links between economic growth and employment growth. Others have already sought explanations of why the traditional link between economic growth and employment creation appears to have weakened in recent years. As the OECD's *Employment Outlook* of July 1990 put it,

> unemployment rates in many OECD countries are generally higher than they were a decade ago, despite seven consecutive years of economic growth and a slower growing youth population. There have been numerous explanations advanced to account for this phenomenon, among them increased structural change, decreased mobility of labour, employer reluctance to hire and a skill shortfall among the unemployed in the face of technological change. In some countries, changes in unemployment insurance regulations are believed to have contributed to a rise in the 'natural' rate of unemployment.   X

The principal focus of this book will be an examination of the cost to employers of employing people and the returns to employees from work and other income-earning activity. The underlying argument is that over the past decade these costs have been pushed progressively further apart by the operation of budgetary and taxation policy. The growing size of this tax wedge, until recently at least, has inhibited the labour market from working either effectively or efficiently. As a result, even when output growth has been strong, employment growth has been weak.

The need to capitalise in employment terms on periods of high growth is brought home with renewed force by the experience of the early 1990s when economic activity faltered at home and abroad. Recession in Britain and the United States from mid-1990 onwards caused a contraction in the foreign employment opportunities available to potential Irish emigrants. In the year to mid-April 1991, net emigration from Ireland fell to just 1,000. With weaker levels of economic activity at home causing domestic job creation to stall, the sharp decline in emigration allied to continuous growth in the domestic labour supply forced unemployment up to the highest level ever recorded in Ireland during the course of 1991.

WHAT PEOPLE EARN IN IRELAND

It is a commonly held view that Americans, being a confessional people, will reveal on early acquaintance the most intimate details of their personal lives—save one: how much they earn. Irish statistics are somewhat similar. The Central Statistics Office produces a wide array of the most useful information, delving into many arcane spheres in search of quantifiable knowledge. There are statistics on the total floor area of buildings for which planning permission has been granted each quarter; there are figures on the electricity output of generating stations each month measured in gigawatts; the number of pigs slaughtered each month is enumerated. But nowhere does the CSO produce figures for average employee incomes. As a result, no concrete information exists on how much the average Irish employee earns.

Much piecemeal data on earnings is collected assiduously. Highly aggregated figures for total personal incomes from all sources are available in each year's national income accounts. But in between there is nothing. The absence of a consistent series on employee incomes, even for those engaged in non-agricultural activity, is a source of two important difficulties. First, it is difficult to track with any precision what is happening to rates of pay increases in the economy, a piece of information that would prove useful to many people engaged in economic policy-making. Second, it is difficult to assess in any detail the impact of changes in personal taxation and social insurance on personal disposable incomes.

When people speak of 'average earnings' in Ireland they are usually referring to average earnings in industry, a category for which consistent statistics are available over a long period. This series, *Industrial Earnings and Hours Worked*, is derived from a quarterly survey of industrial employers. With some 1,300 respondent firms, the survey covers roughly 130,000 industrial employees working in production facilities employing more than twenty people. However, since there are more than 950,000 people at work in Ireland outside agriculture, the average

Table 5

Average weekly earnings in manufacturing industry and construction, 1979–90

Gross weekly earnings from all sources including overtime and bonuses in £s at current money values

	(1)	(2)	(3)	(4)	(5)	(6)
Year	All industrial workers in manufacturing	Male industrial workers in manufacturing	Managerial workers in industry	Clerical workers in industry	Skilled building workers in the private sector	Unskilled/ semiskilled building workers
1979	81.41	96.62	n.c.	n.c.		
1980	96.20	113.11	n.c.	n.c.	121.71	107.51
1981	112.25	131.55	n.c.	n.c.	141.99	124.02
1982	126.69	147.52	224.22	140.49	167.42	144.55
1983	141.55	164.58	255.86	160.78	175.50	149.42
1984	158.79	184.40	283.17	177.39	190.31	162.81
1985	171.45	201.98	303.96	186.83	195.86	166.72
1986	184.24	216.66	325.62	201.99	202.40	172.72
1987	193.64	227.30	346.91	214.97	205.55	172.82
1988	202.82	237.69	365.41	225.77	212.01	183.35
1989	210.98	247.86	381.54	237.64	221.49	191.97
1990	217.59	255.64	393.89	248.78	228.85	197.53

n.c.: Not collected. All earnings figures for 1990 represent final figures for June 1990.
Notes and sources: (1) Average weekly earnings of men, women and youths at work in manufacturing industry from *Industrial Earnings and Hours Worked* (quarterly), CSO.
(2) Male industrial workers in manufacturing industry only. Columns 1 and 2 relate to operatives or factory-floor workers only.
(3) In 1982, 1983 and 1984 these figures were collected for September only. Thereafter they were collected quarterly, and the figures from 1985 onwards are averages for four quarters. These figures cover managerial workers in industry only.
(4) Coverage and compilation the same as column 3. Note that 3 and 4 are calculated separately from 1 and 2, and are thus wholly independent of the averages for 1 and 2.
(5–6) Derived from a quarterly sample of *Average Earnings and Hours Worked* [*Building Industry*] (CSO)

earnings of industrial employees cannot be taken as indicative of average earnings among all non-agricultural employees.

The figures for average industrial earnings relate to the weekly earnings of operatives and factory-floor workers, including overtime and bonuses. In addition, annually since 1982 and quarterly since 1985, the quarterly industrial inquiry has collected separate sets of earnings data for clerical and managerial employees in industry. Since 1980 the construction section within the CSO has collected quarterly earnings data for skilled operatives and for semi-skilled and unskilled workers in private-sector building and construction. No industry-wide data on earnings in the services sector is collected, although an index of earnings in financial services was instituted in March 1988; this is computed quarterly. In summary, there are relatively complete series for earnings in industry and for private sector earnings in building and construction; but the collection of earnings data in the services sector is at an embryonic stage.

The most important sets of data for employee earnings in industry and construction are summarised in table 5 for the years 1979 to 1989, where available. As can be seen from the table, average earnings for all industrial workers—men, women, and youths—in manufacturing industry rose from a weekly level of £81.41 in 1979 to £210.98 in 1989. This represented a gross earnings gain of 159 per cent over the ten-year period. From the viewpoint of this study the most important message contained in table 5 is the extent to which average industrial earnings in manufacturing industry *understated* the average earnings of other private-sector employees. Thus in 1982, the first year for which earnings data was available for all categories surveyed, the average weekly earnings of all industrial workers lay below those of unskilled and semi-skilled building workers, clerical workers in industry, skilled building operatives, and managerial employees. While interesting shifts in pay relativities occurred between 1982 and 1989, by the latter year average weekly earnings in industry still lay below the earnings of clerical workers in industry, skilled construction workers, and managerial employees in industry.

Thus, while average industrial earnings are conventionally used as the benchmark for the absolute earnings of all employees, it cannot be taken for granted that these are a reliable indicator of average employee earnings; the evidence in table 5 suggests that average industrial earnings understate the average earnings even of those engaged as employees in industry and construction.

Further corroboration of this view can be adduced from the results of annual labour force surveys and of the annual national income and expenditure accounts. The number of non-agricultural employees at work each year can be derived from the CSO's labour force survey. The national income and expenditure accounts for each year show the aggregate level of non-agricultural employee remuneration. By dividing the total number of non-agricultural employees into total non-agricultural employee remuneration, a set of figures for average non-agricultural employee remuneration can be derived.

On the basis of sample surveys, estimates of the total number of non-agricultural employees are made each April by the CSO. (From 1975 to 1983 these labour force surveys were

Table 6					
Numbers of agricultural and non-agricultural employees and their relationship to totals at work, 1979–89 (000)					
Year (mid-April)	Total at work	Total employees	of which:	Agricultural employees	Non-agricultural
1989	1,090	825.3		22.3	803.0
1988	1,091	823.6		24.3	799.3
1987	1,080	828.8		24.4	804.4
1986	1,081	830.6		25.2	805.4
1985	1,079	819.8		23.0	796.8
1984	1,103	832.2		21.1	811.1
1983	1,124	849.2		21.5	827.7
1982	1,146	n.a.		n.a.	n.a
1981	1,146	877.9		24.3	853.6
1980	1,156	n.a.		n.a.	n.a.
1979	1,150	855.2		27.6	827.6

Sources: Labour Force Survey, 1979; '5% Sample of 1981 Census of Population'; Labour Force Surveys 1983 to 1989, as revised. The author would like to thank Mr Bill O'Gorman of the Labour Force Survey section in the CSO for his assistance in reconciling the figures for employees with the LFS revisions for the totals at work in 1983, 1984, and 1985.
Notes: n.a.: Not available (no breakdowns are available for 1980 or 1982, as no labour force surveys were undertaken in those years).

Table 7

Trends in non-agricultural employee remuneration, 1979–89

Year	Non-agricultural employee remuneration (£ million)	Number of non-agricultural employees (000)	Average annual remuneration £	Remuneration per week £
1979	4,193.9	827.6	5,067.54	97.45
1980	5,200.4	n.a.	(6,143.25)	(118.14)
1981	6,162.1	853.6	7,218.96	138.83
1982	6,988.8	n.a.	(8,213.14)	(157.95)
1983	7,620.9	827.7	9,207.32	177.06
1984	8,251.1	811.1	10,172.73	195.63
1985	8,740.3	796.8	10,969.25	210.95
1986	9,293.2	805.4	11,538.61	221.90
1987	9,802.3	804.4	12,185.85	234.34
1988	10,272	799.3	12,851.24	247.14
1989	10,944	803.0	13,628.89	262.09

Note: n.a.: Not available. Non-agricultural employee remuneration is as shown in item 10 of the national accounts: 'Non-agricultural income: Remuneration of employees: Wages, salaries and pensions'. This item includes earnings from all sources, including bonuses, overtime, piecework payments, and commissions and fees arising from economic activity within the state. Income in kind is also included. Transfer payments such as old-age pensions and unemployment benefits are excluded. Pensions paid to former employees are also excluded, except where such pensions are unfunded. In the case of funded pension schemes, employers' contributions are included in this item. The figures for pay should thus be regarded as the annual value of the 'total remuneration package' rather than simple 'earnings'.

Sources: *National Income and Expenditure, 1986, 1987, 1988, 1989*, Central Statistics Office. The data on the number of employees is taken from table 6.

conducted every two years, but from 1983 onwards they were undertaken annually.) As shown in table 6, there were over 800,000 non-agricultural employees at work in Ireland in 1989 out of a total work force of 1.09 million. The proportion of the work force accounted for by employees has remained remarkably stable over time, at around 75 per cent of the total.

The national income and expenditure tables published each year by the CSO provide aggregate data for the remuneration of domestic non-agricultural employees. Dividing the totals for non-agricultural employees, as shown in table 6, into the aggregate levels of non-agricultural employee remuneration, a series of estimates is obtained for non-agricultural employee remuneration for the years 1979 to 1989; these calculations are shown in table 7. Where no data was available on the number of non-agricultural employees because no labour force survey was taken that year, as in 1980 and 1982, estimates for annual employee remuneration outside agriculture have been inter-polated. There is an additional complication. The figures for aggregate employee remuneration as calculated by the CSO include employers' contributions to employee pension plans, and pension payments to former employees where such pensions were unfunded. The average non-agricultural remu-neration shown for each year in table 7 thus overstates the amount of gross cash income received by employees, perhaps by as much as 10 per cent.

Even allowing this caveat, there is still a striking difference between the figures for average non-agricultural employee remuneration as shown in table 7 and the figures for average earnings in manufacturing industry as shown in table 5 (column 1). In all cases, the national accounts estimates for average employee incomes throughout the economy are consistently higher than the corresponding figures for average industrial earnings in each of the years surveyed. This reinforces the con-tention that *non-agricultural employee incomes are significantly higher on average than industrial earnings in manufacturing industry.*

Thus, for example, in 1989 average weekly earnings for all industrial workers in manufacturing industry came to £210.98. In the same year, and calculated on a national accounts basis, average employee incomes throughout the non-agricultural economy stood at £262.09 a week. The gap between the two figures—£51.11 a week, or almost one-quarter of average man-ufacturing earnings—seems too large to be accounted for by the more expansive national accounts definition of non-agricultural employee remuneration.

On the—admittedly incomplete—evidence available, it would appear that the trend in average non-agricultural employee pay approximates more closely to average *male* industrial earnings in manufacturing than to the average earnings of all industrial workers. At the very least it is clear that average industrial earnings in manufacturing—the figure most commonly associated in the public mind with 'average pay'—understates consistently the actual level of employee earnings throughout the non-agricultural economy.

An important conclusion follows. Since the Irish income tax code is highly progressive, with tax rates rising steeply as incomes increase, and since average employee incomes are significantly higher than average industrial earnings in manufacturing (the usual basis for calculation of the extent of the income tax burden), then both the average weight of that burden and the size of the tax wedge are bigger than is usually conceded.

PAY VERSUS PRICES

3

Modern money has no intrinsic worth; its value derives exclusively from the power it confers on individuals to buy goods and services. So too with money incomes. The value of a weekly pay-packet or monthly cheque is not determined by the amount of gross income earned but by the spending power of take-home pay. In the last analysis, employees are not interested only in the gross pay they earn, for the simple reason that they never actually receive it. Instead it is the purchasing power of take-home pay—gross income less taxes and other deductions—that is of fundamental financial importance to employees.

Three separate factors interact to determine the real spending power of pay. First of all, the level of gross pay itself, and the extent to which it increases from year to year, governs the ability to spend. But trends in pay increases over time are not by themselves an accurate guide to the improvement in employees' purchasing power, for it is not only incomes that rise from year to year: prices facing consumers also increase. Thus the second determinant of purchasing power is the level of inflation. Increases in prices whittle away the value of pay rises, eroding real purchasing power. If prices are rising faster than pay, real purchasing power will decline. Consumers then find themselves in the uncomfortable position of being worse off even as their money incomes are rising. It is essential, therefore, to adjust trends in money incomes to take account of concurrent changes in prices, the result being *real income*.

Even an adjustment for changes in prices does not give us the full picture, however. Deductions in the form of income taxes, training levies and health and social insurance contributions are made from incomes before they are handed over to employees; thus money incomes have to be adjusted not only for changes in prices but also for changes in the weight of the personal tax burden before the full shape of employees' spending power can be delineated.

When money incomes are adjusted to take account both of changes in prices and changes in personal taxes over time, the

Table 8 (a)

Indices of employee earnings and consumer prices, 1980–90

1980 = 100

Year	Average earnings in manufacturing	Average male earnings in manufacturing	Average employee remuneration	Skilled building workers' average earnings	Consumer prices
1980	100	100	100	100	100
1981	116.7	116.3	117.5	116.7	120.4
1982	131.7	130.4	133.7	137.6	141.0
1983	147.1	145.5	149.9	144.2	155.8
1984	165.1	163.0	165.6	156.4	169.2
1985	178.2	178.6	178.6	160.9	178.4
1986	191.5	191.5	187.8	166.3	185.2
1987	201.3	201.0	198.4	168.9	191.0
1988	210.8	210.1	209.2	174.2	195.1
1989	219.3	219.1	221.9	182.0	203.1
1990 (mid-year)	226.2	226.0	n.a.	188.0	208.8

Table 8 (b)

Annual percentage changes in employee earnings and consumer prices, 1980–90

1981	16.7	16.3	17.5	16.7	20.4
1982	12.9	12.1	13.8	17.9	17.2
1983	11.7	11.6	12.1	4.8	10.5
1984	12.2	12.0	10.5	8.5	8.6
1985	8.0	9.5	7.8	2.9	5.4
1986	7.5	7.3	5.2	3.3	3.9
1987	5.1	4.9	5.6	1.6	3.2
1988	4.7	4.6	5.5	3.1	2.1
1989	4.0	4.3	6.1	4.5	4.1
1990 (mid-year)	3.1	3.1	n.a.	3.3	2.8

n.a. = Not available.
Sources: Calculations based on data in tables 5 and 7, 'Consumer Price Index', Central Statistics Office. See also *Economic Review and Outlook, 1990*, Department of Finance, August 1990, tables 15 and 16.

results represent *real disposable incomes*. It is such real after-tax incomes that establish individuals' purchasing power: their command over goods and services.

Absolute earnings for a range of different employments were shown in table 5, augmented by a series of overall estimates of employee remuneration during the 1980s illustrated in table 7. These tables show not only the average level of earnings in different jobs in particular years but changes in average earnings from year to year. Earnings in money terms escalated rapidly during the 1980s. Judged in isolation, it might be concluded that employees' purchasing power and living standards were enhanced greatly as a result. But this was not the case: both inflation and a weightier personal tax burden exacted heavy charges on the rise in cash incomes throughout the decade. Trends in real spending power, therefore, cannot be derived from trends in money incomes alone, without taking account of the other two factors that determine purchasing power: rising prices and heavier taxes. To focus solely on changes in money incomes is to be guilty of 'money illusion'.

Using the data in tables 5 and 7, table 8 (*a*) shows trends in average earnings for a range of employments in the form of index numbers, with 1980 as the base in each case. This makes clearer the movements in money incomes over the decade. By introducing a consumer price index, also with 1980 as the base, we can see the corrosive effects of rising prices on rising pay quite clearly. Table 8 (*b*) restates the data in table 8 (*a*) in terms of year-to-year percentage changes.

As can be seen from table 8 (*a*), the average money earnings of most employees rose by a factor of two-and-a-quarter between 1980 and 1990. The exception was the building trade, where growth in earnings was much lower, because of depressed conditions for most of the decade. These gains might have been expected to herald a significant leap forward in living standards during the decade. They did not. Inflation intruded, absorbing most of the spending power conferred by rising money incomes. As shown, average consumer prices more than doubled during the decade, thus allowing only modest gains in real incomes during the 1980s, with these concentrated heavily in the final years of the decade.

On the basis of the index data shown in table 8 (*a*), table 8 (*b*) shows year-to-year changes in earnings and prices in percentage terms for the 1980s. As can be seen, consumer price inflation decelerated sharply and continuously throughout the decade. The inflation rate in 1988 was just one-tenth of what it had been seven years earlier. The annual increase in consumer prices has not exceeded 5 per cent since 1985. Earnings growth decelerated in sympathy with the slow-down in consumer price inflation through the 1980s, though not quite as quickly. However, by the final years of the decade pay and price increases were marching almost in step.

Some tentative conclusions can be drawn from the data in these tables. First, both annual rates of inflation in consumer prices and the pace of pay rises were much lower at the end of the decade than they had been at its beginning. But the moderation in earnings growth followed the weakening of inflationary pressures. This suggests that inflation plays a decisive part in determining the rate of pay growth. Where prices are rising rapidly, employees will seek compensation for the erosion in the purchasing power of their earnings by demanding higher pay. In most cases earnings appear to track inflation, but with a lag. Throughout the 1980s the rate of inflation declined first; the rate of earnings growth decelerated later.

Second, there was a considerable degree of uniformity in the annual rates of earnings increase recorded by different categories of workers. In broad terms, average earnings of all industrial workers in manufacturing, average male manufacturing earnings and the average employee remuneration figures from the national accounts all exhibited roughly the same pace of earnings growth from year to year. This also holds true for earnings of administrative and clerical workers in industry and for managerial employees, though these are not illustrated here. This broad uniformity held, not just over the decade as a whole but from year to year. In consequence there was a general tendency for pay relativities to be maintained during the 1980s—whether or not national pay agreements were in operation. However, there were exceptions to this general scheme of things. One of the most notable was the case of skilled workers in private-sector construction, whose earnings increased only two-thirds as fast as those of average industrial employees in manufacturing. Building workers' earnings lagged significantly behind inflation during the 1980s. The reasons for this are not difficult to fathom. The building and construction sector suffered a deep depression in the years between the early and late 1980s; unemployment in the sector rose sharply in consequence, and depressed levels of activity and rising unemployment curbed the rate of growth of basic pay. In addition, the relatively

Table 9

Trends in average earnings, personal taxes, consumer prices, and real consumer spending, 1980–90

1980 = 100

Year	(1) Average earnings	(2) Personal taxes	(3) Consumer prices	(4) Real personal consumer spending on goods and services
1980	100	100	100	100
1981	116.7	123.2	120.4	101.7
1982	131.7	151.2	141.0	94.6
1983	147.1	178.9	155.8	95.4
1984	165.1	212.1	169.2	97.3
1985	178.2	225.1	178.4	100.7
1986	191.5	247.3	185.2	102.7
1987	201.3	276.7	191.0	105.0
1988	210.8	312.2	195.1	107.7
1989	219.3	292.1	203.1	113.2
1990*	226.2	313.8	208.8	116.9

*For 1990 the figures for average earnings relate to the end of June 1990, and the consumer price indices relate to mid-May 1990. The personal taxes index reflects the calendar year tax yield for 1990, while real consumer spending in 1990 is based on Department of Finance estimates.

Notes: (1) Average earnings shown represent average earnings of all industrial workers in manufacturing industry. Here these are used as a proxy for trends in employee earnings throughout the economy.
(2) The personal taxes index is based on revenues collected from income tax, employees' social insurance contributions (including health contributions), the 1% income levy, and the 1% youth employment levy (employment and training levy). The 1988 index reflects that year's tax amnesty.
(3) This is the consumer price index re-based to 1980 = 100.
(4) This index is derived from table A of the National Income and Expenditure tables, 1989. It has been updated for 1990 by the inclusion of the Department of Finance's estimate for personal consumer spending growth that year.

sluggish rate of earnings growth reflected a paring back of overtime and bonuses; this would suggest that there is a limit to the extent to which employees can succeed in winning compensation for increases in consumer prices through related rises in earnings: where labour market conditions are particularly depressed, such indexed compensation will not be forthcoming.

Third, for all but building workers, gross earnings grew faster than prices during the 1980s. The extent to which earnings growth outpaced inflation might be taken as an indicator of the width of the potential gain in material living standards over the decade. However, this would be to neglect the effects of a rising personal tax burden—the third element in the purchasing power equation. The effects of the twin attacks mounted by heavier personal taxes and rising prices on money earnings during the 1980s are illustrated in table 9. Again, for the sake of expositional clarity the trends in each case are represented by index numbers with a common base in 1980. As can be seen, gross average earnings in manufacturing industry—standing here as a proxy for trends in average earnings throughout the economy—increased by a factor of two-and-a-quarter during the decade. But personal income taxes rose even faster. The yield from income tax more than doubled between 1980 and 1984; between 1980 and 1990 direct taxes on personal incomes more than tripled. Personal income taxes are defined here as income tax, employees' health and social insurance contributions, the 1 per cent income levy, and the 1 per cent youth employment levy, later the employment and training levy.

With tax on personal income taking an ever-bigger bite out of rising employee earnings—a trend that was reversed only in the final years of the decade—the growth in after-tax, disposable income was stunted. And it was with these incomes depleted by higher taxes that employees faced rising prices in the shops. Between 1980 and the middle of 1990, consumer prices more than doubled.

The results were inevitable. In the first half of the 1980s, when inflation was at its most rapid and income taxes were rising very fast, real consumer spending on goods and services fell sharply. Rising unemployment, falling numbers at work and an increase in national savings born out of fear of the future all contributed to a decline in real consumer spending of 5 per cent in 1982 and 1983 compared with 1980. It was not until 1985 that real consumer spending surpassed the levels attained in 1980.

As inflation abated and the annual increases in personal tax impositions became less punishing in the second half of the decade, consumer spending in volume terms began to show

Table 10

Effects of rising taxes and inflation on the evolution of personal incomes, 1980–90

(£million at current prices unless otherwise stated)

Year	Personal incomes	Taxes on personal incomes	Personal disposable incomes	Consumer price index (1980 =100)	Real personal disposable income, (1980 prices)	Effective personal tax rate (%)	Savings as percentage of personal disposable incomes
1980	8,821	1,486	7,335	100	7,335	16.8	16.0
1981	10,828	1,829	8,999	120.4	7,490	16.9	16.8
1982	12,310	2,273	10,037	141.0	7,118	18.5	20.3
1983	13,523	2,665	10,858	155.8	6,969	19.7	18.8
1984	14,917	3,123	11,794	169.2	6,970	20.9	18.2
1985	15,831	3,332	12,499	178.4	7,006	21.0	16.1
1986	16,895	3,625	13,270	185.2	7,165	21.5	15.8
1987	18,282	3,999	14,283	191.0	7,478	21.9	17.5
1988	18,998	4,463*	14,535	195.1	7,450	23.5	14.9
1989e	20,109	4,323	15,786	203.1	7,773	21.5	14.3
1990e	21,305	4,647	16,658	210.0	7,932	21.8	14.0
Change 1980—90	141.5%	212.7%	127.1%	110.0%	8.1%	29.8%	−12.5%

* The personal tax yield in 1988, and thus the effective personal tax rate, was inflated by receipts flowing from that year's tax amnesty.
Sources: Data on personal incomes and personal taxes, 1980–88, were derived from *National Income and Expenditure, 1987, 1988, 1989*. The estimates for 1989 and 1990 are as shown by the Economic and Social Research Institute in table 9 of its *Quarterly Economic Commentary*, December 1990. These figures are computed on a national accounts basis.

signs of a revival. The gradual improvement in economic conditions as the decade neared its end prompted a reduction in personal savings. These factors combined to engineer a modest consumer boom in the final years of the decade. Nonetheless, for the period as a whole, real consumer spending increased by less than 17 per cent—poor value for a rise of more than 125 per cent in gross average earnings between 1980 and 1990. Price rises and tax increases had combined to take most of the good out of the substantial increases in nominal money incomes.

A wider economic perspective is adopted in table 10. This shows the effects of rising prices and of *all* taxes on personal incomes on the evolution of total personal income in the economy during the 1980s. The definition of personal income adopted here is more extensive. In addition to employee income, it includes personal income derived from rents, dividends, and interest; only the income of public authorities and the undistributed profits of companies are excluded. Similarly, the definition of personal taxes has been broadened to include all social insurance contributions and deposit interest retention tax.

This aggregate data for the economy as a whole confirms the depressing effects exerted by rising prices and higher taxes on real personal disposable income. These effects were particularly noticeable in the first half of the 1980s. Personal incomes in money terms rose from £8,800 million in 1980 to an estimated £21,300 million in 1990; this represented an increase of 141.5 per cent in personal income over the decade. During these years taxes on personal incomes rose from £1,500 million to £4,600 million, an increase of 212.7 per cent. As a result, the effective rates at which personal income was taxed rose by five percentage points over the ten-year period. The effective tax rate borne by personal incomes stood at 16.8 per cent in 1980; by 1990 it had risen to 21.8 per cent. The increase in the weight of the personal tax burden over the decade held back the rate of growth in after-tax disposable incomes. While gross personal incomes rose by 141.5 per cent between 1980 and 1990, the increase in disposable money incomes amounted to just 127.1 per cent.

It was not only rising taxes that confiscated purchasing power. Consumer prices also rose rapidly, particularly in the first half of the decade. Between 1980 and 1986 consumer prices rose by 85 per cent, while for the decade as a whole, average prices in the shops increased by 110 per cent. When after-tax incomes are adjusted for changes in prices, it can be seen that real personal disposable income—real purchasing power—suffered a significant decline during the mid-1980s. Real personal spending power in the economy began to decline after 1981, and fell continuously until 1985. As measured by real disposable personal incomes, spending power did not again exceed the levels attained in 1981 until 1989. This slump in real incomes provides a convincing explanation for the weakness of real consumer spending during the middle years of the 1980s, as shown in table 9; people simply did not have the money to spend.

Another force was also at work. As economic conditions deteriorated in the early 1980s, people began to build up their savings as insurance against an uncertain future. Since incomes can only be spent or saved, this sharp increase in personal savings was achieved at the expense of further reductions in personal consumption. As economic conditions improved in the second half of the decade, people felt confident enough to begin running down their very high levels of precautionary savings, allocating more to spending and less to saving. The sharp rise in the personal savings ratio during the early 1980s had accelerated the down-turn in consumer spending during those years. Conversely, reductions in personal savings in the latter years of the decade gave a further fillip to personal consumption growth. The modest consumer boom of the last years of the 1980s was financed to a significant extent by a collective decision to switch from saving to spending.

The central lesson of the 1980s was that real personal disposable incomes could fall even as money incomes were registering apparently healthy gains. The experience of the 1980s also taught that a rapid escalation of the personal tax burden together with rising prices were the principal agents of the destruction of purchasing power. The realisation among employees that the confiscatory effects of inflation and taxes are similar in nature may have released a set of dynamic effects. Just as rising prices can induce claims for compensation in the form of higher pay, so too can additions to the weight of the personal tax burden trigger compensatory pay claims. Put another way, the ultimate financial objective of income earners is to preserve, and if possible enhance, real purchasing power. Where this is eroded by rising effective personal tax rates, precisely the same defensive response will be elicited among employees as when they are confronted with rising prices.

THE WEIGHTY BURDEN OF PERSONAL TAX IN THE 1980s

4

The greater part of the 1980s were years of high taxes and low economic growth. In broad terms, the yield from income and payroll taxes tripled in the course of the decade, while GNP, measured in money terms, increased by a factor of two-and-a-half. As a result, income taxes increased their share of GNP significantly during the 1980s.

Personal incomes were subjected to four separate forms of tax during the last decade, two old, two new. The existing taxes charged on personal incomes were income tax proper and employees' pay-related social insurance (PRSI) contributions. However, in the course of the decade these were augmented by two new income levies, the 1 per cent youth employment levy (later renamed the employment and training levy) and the 1 per cent income levy; the latter was discontinued in 1986. The combined yield from these taxes on income was equivalent to 12.9 per cent of GNP in 1980; a decade later their share of GNP had risen by more than three percentage points, to 16.2 per cent.

Taxes on personal incomes paid by income-earners are not the only forms of direct taxes levied on income. In addition, employers pay social insurance contributions on behalf of their employees; the proceeds of these contributions are used to fund employee benefits. These payroll taxes charged to employers also rose appreciably during the decade, increasing from £305 million in 1980 to an estimated £876 million in 1990. Taken together, income and payroll taxes increased from 16.3 per cent of GNP in 1980 to reach 20 per cent in 1990. (The trend in income taxes over the last decade is illustrated in table 11.)

The taxing experience that was the 1980s can be subdivided into two distinct segments. In the period 1980 to 1986 the economy virtually stood still. At the same time the direct tax burden was made much weightier; in consequence, income taxes rose appreciably as a proportion of GNP, increasing from 12.9 per cent in 1980 to 17.1 per cent by 1986. Income and payroll taxes

Table 11

Income and payroll taxes, 1980–90
(£ million at current prices)

	1980	1981	1982	1983	1984	1985	1986	1987	1988	1989	1990
Income tax	1,013	1,246	1,458	1,661	1,968	2,105	2,383	2,718	3,046	2,831	3,028*
Employees' PRSI	150	187	263	310	337	355	369	400	455	470	500*
1% employment and training levy	0	0	38	70	84	84	91	97	125	117	125
1% income levy	0	0	0	40	78	74	33	3	5	0	0
Total employee income taxes	1,163	1,433	1,759	2,081	2,467	2,618	2,876	3,218	3,631	3,418	3,653*
Employers' PRSI	305	375	475	534	598	649	680	710	758	829	876*
Total income and payroll taxes	1,468	1,808	2,234	2,615	3,065	3,267	3,556	3,928	4,389	4,247	4,529
GNP	9,003	10,854	12,455	13,595	14,768	15,725	16,780	18,084	18,940	20,879	22,600
Employee income taxes as percentage of GNP	12.9	13.2	14.1	15.3	16.7	16.6	17.1	17.8	19.2	16.4	16.2
Total income and payroll taxes as percentage of GNP	16.3	16.7	17.9	19.2	20.8	20.8	21.2	21.7	23.2	20.4	20.0
MEMORANDUM ITEMS:											
Total PRSI	455	562	738	844	935	1,004	1,049	1,110	1,213	1,299	1,376
Corporation tax	140	200	232	215	210	218	258	256	334	303	474

* estimate

Notes: The tax yields and proportionate tax rates for 1988 were inflated by the proceeds of the tax amnesty that year. This yielded an estimated additional £500 million in collected revenue. The PRSI contributions of the self-employed—£46 million in 1989—have been aggregated with those of employers.

Sources: *Budget, 1980–90*; *Principal Features of 1991 Budget*; *National Income and Expenditure, 1986–89* (CSO).

taken together exhibited a similar trend, rising from 16.3 to 21.2 per cent of GNP over this period.

Economic conditions changed in 1987, when vibrant economic growth returned. Initially, however, the resurgence of growth did not prompt any reductions in income and payroll taxes. The incoming Minister for Finance, Ray MacSharry, left tax rates, bands and allowances broadly unchanged, using the increased tax yields generated by growth to reduce the size of the public sector deficit. As a result, income taxes rose to 17.8 per cent of GNP in 1987, while combined income and payroll taxes increased their share of GNP to 21.7 per cent.

At first sight, the tax yields for 1988 might be taken as indicating a further tax imposition on personal incomes, a further raising of effective income tax rates. However, while the revenues accruing to the exchequer did increase significantly during 1988, the source of these additional tax flows was not a rise in current tax rates but the repayment of past taxes without penalty under that year's tax amnesty. When extraordinary, once-off revenues accruing under the amnesty are excluded from 1988 tax receipts, personal income taxes as a proportion of GNP actually *declined* between 1987 and 1988. As a share of GNP, underlying current personal tax revenues reached a peak in 1987, and declined modestly in succeeding years. From 1988 onwards, income tax rates were reduced, bands were widened, and basic allowances were increased. But it is necessary to retain a sense of proportion about the degree of progress achieved since 1988. While the personal tax take has fallen from the peaks it scaled in 1987/88, effective income tax rates remain much higher now than they were in 1980.

The rise in the tax burden imposed on personal incomes did not come about as the result of a single policy change. Rather, the heavier tax burden resulted on the one hand from the accretion of small incremental changes in the tax code and on the other hand from the absence of sufficient change. The latter might appear somewhat paradoxical; but the refusal of governments to allow sufficiently for the effects of inflation when framing their budgets in effect transforms inflation itself into an instrument of taxation. Especially in the early years of the 1980s, when prices were rising rapidly, inflation acted as an extremely effective, but handily disguised, mode of raising additional revenue for the exchequer.

Piecemeal changes are the hallmark of annual budgets; innovations are infrequent. It is extremely difficult to summarise the incremental changes in personal taxes effected on a year-to-year

Table 12

Evolution of personal taxation, 1980/81–1991/92

Category	1980/81	1981/82	1982/83	1983/84	1984/85	1985/86	1986/87	1987/88	1988/89	1989/90	1990/91	1991/92	Change 1980–91	Inflation
1. Basic tax allowances:														
– Single person (£)	1,515	1,715	2,362	2,336	2,686	2,786	2,986	2,986	3,136	3,136	3,136	3,186	110.3%	130.5%
– Married couple, one spouse working (£)	3,020	3,220	4,012	3,986	4,686	4,886	4,986	4,986	5,186	5,186	5,186	5,286	75.0%	130.5%
2. Tax rates:														
– Number of income tax rates	5	5	5	6	5	3	3	3	3	3	3	3	–2	
– Lowest income tax rate (%)	25	25	25	25	35	35	35	35	35	32	30	29	plus 4 percentage points	
– Standard income tax rate (%)	35	35	35	35	35	35	35	35	35	32	30	29	minus 6 percentage points	
– Highest income tax rate (%)	60	60	60	65	65	60	58	58	58	56	53	52	minus 8 percentage points	
3. Income tax bands:														
– Taxable income threshold for exposure to tax at higher rates:														
– Single person (£)	5,000	5,500	4,000	4,000	4,000	4,500	4,700	4,700	5,700	6,100	6,500	6,700	34.0%	130.5%
– Married couple (£)	10,000	11,000	8,000	8,000	8,000	9,000	9,400	9,400	11,400	12,200	13,000	13,400	34.0%	130.5%
– Taxable income threshold for exposure to tax at highest rates:														
– Single person (£)	9,000	9,500	8,000	10,000	10,000	7,300	7,500	7,500	8,600	9,200	9,600	9,800	8.9%	130.5%
– Married couple (£)	18,000	19,000	16,000	20,000	20,000	14,600	15,000	15,000	17,200	18,400	19,200	19,600	8.9%	130.5%
4. Other income taxes:														
– Employees' PRSI, levies charged on gross income (%)	4.5	4.75	7.5	8.5	8.5	8.5	7.5	7.75	7.75	7.75	7.75	7.75	plus 3.25 percentage points	
– Employers' PRSI charged on gross employee income (%)	9.80	10.25	11.61	11.61	12.1	12.2	12.33	12.33	12.4	12.2	12.2	12.2	plus 2.4 percentage points	

Notes: (1) Basic tax allowances included the standard allowance and the PAYE and PRSI tax allowances. In the case of a married couple it is assumed that only one spouse is working and that the couple have two children, qualifying for the child tax allowance when applicable.
(2) The lowest and standard tax rates were merged in 1984/85.
(3) This section shows the amount of taxable income above which the taxpaying unit is (a) exposed to income tax at rates above the standard income tax rate and (b) exposed to tax at the highest rate.
(4) In the case of the employee, other income taxes include full-rate PRSI and health contributions, the youth employment levy (employment and training levy) and the 1% income levy. The employer PRSI rates shown are the full rates, on aggregation.

Source: Revenue Commissioners. The author would like to thank Mr Norman Gillanders for supplying the data on which this table is based.

basis over the span of more than a decade. However, since the growing weight of the personal tax burden during the 1980s was the product of many seemingly innocuous changes, an attempt has been made to codify these changes in table 12.

Since the changes in tax allowances and tax bands are couched in current money terms, they do not convey fully the manner in which inflation acted as a phantom tax collector for the exchequer over these years. The money changes in tax allowances and the width of tax bands are thus evaluated in table 12 against the yardstick of consumer price inflation over the period. With a base of November 1975 equalling 100, the consumer price index rose from 173.5 in February 1980 to 399.9 in February 1991. Thus over the whole period average consumer prices rose by 130.5 per cent. To measure the Government's use of inflation as a hidden tax, budgetary changes in tax bands and allowances over the period must be sized against this measure of inflation. It should be noted also that the inflation rate bridging the budgets of 1980 and 1991 spans a longer period than the total inflation rate for 1980–90 shown in table 10.

The growing weight of the personal income tax burden over the eleven-year period from 1980/81 to 1991/92 was accounted for by the interaction of four principal factors. These are summarised below.

1. The sub-indexation of basic tax allowances. Over the period 1980/81 to 1991/92, basic, non-discretionary tax allowances were not increased in line with inflation. As a result of this continuous process of sub-indexation, an increasing proportion of gross income was exposed to tax. Governments have made particular use of sub-indexation as a revenue-raising weapon in recent years; between 1986/87 and 1991/92 the personal tax allowance for a single employee was increased by a mere £200. However, over the period as a whole, married couples with children fared worst of all. Between 1980/81 and 1991/92 the basic tax allowance for married couples with two children lagged behind inflation by 55.5 percentage points where one spouse was working. A large slice of this shortfall was attributable to the withdrawal of automatic tax allowances for children in the tax year of 1986/87.

Single employees fared somewhat better. Over the period as a whole, the increase in their tax allowances—including the PAYE and PRSI tax allowances—came to 110 per cent, some twenty percentage points behind inflation.

The tax allowance computations in table 12 may understate the extent of individuals' increased exposure to income tax in two respects. Firstly, the computations assume that employees enjoy access to the special PAYE and PRSI tax allowances, which at present stand at £800 and £286, respectively; where income tax payers cannot claim such allowances, a larger slice of their annual incomes would be exposed to income tax. For 1991/92 the basic tax allowances have been set at £2,100 for single people and £4,200 for married couples.

Secondly, most discretionary tax allowances have been trimmed back since 1980, including the scale of permitted tax relief on mortgage interest payments and on life assurance premiums. Nor should it be forgotten that for personal taxpayers, interest other than mortgage interest no longer qualifies for any form of tax relief. Thus, by refusing to raise the level of basic tax allowances in line with inflation, successive Governments have used rising prices as a hidden instrument of taxation.

2. Changes in tax rates. The low 25 per cent rate of income was abolished in 1984/85; thereafter, the low and standard rates of income tax were fused. For most of the decade the standard rate of income tax remained at 35 per cent. However, reductions in the standard rate were effected in each of the three years from 1989/90 onwards. This rate—the first rate faced by taxpayers on their taxable income—was cut to 32 per cent in 1989/90; a further reduction to 30 per cent followed in 1990/91, while in 1991/92 it was clipped by a further one percentage point to 29 per cent. In 1980/81 there were five rates of income tax, levied progressively on taxable income. Their number rose to six in 1983/84, when a new top rate of 65 per cent was introduced. This lasted only two years, and from 1985/86 the top rate of income tax has moved downwards continuously. For 1991/92 the top rate has been cut to 52 per cent, some thirteen percentage points below its recent peak in 1983–85.

Despite these reductions in income tax rates—more apparent than real in many cases—Ireland's relative standing in the international income tax league has deteriorated in recent years, and for two reasons. Firstly, the abolition of the low 25 per cent rate in 1984/85 meant that income tax payers thereafter paid their first chunk of tax at the standard tax rate. While this standard rate has been reduced from 35 to 29 per cent in the intervening years, the starting rate today is still four percentage points higher than it was a decade ago. This initial rate is very high by international standards. A study published by the OECD in December 1990 found that among its members the first rate payable on taxable income ranged between 1 per cent in Switzerland and 33 per cent in Iceland. Ireland's starting rate of 30 per cent in 1990/91 was thus the second-highest in the industrial world.

Secondly, while the top rate of tax has declined significantly in Ireland over the past five years, it has declined even faster in most other industrial countries. Between 1986 and 1991 the top rate was reduced from 58 to 52 per cent, a cut of six percentage points. In its study *The Public Sector: Issues for the 1990s* the OECD found that between 1986 and 1990 the top rate of income tax was cut by thirty percentage points to 20 per cent in Sweden, by twenty-four percentage points to 33 per cent in New Zealand, and by twenty-two percentage points to 28 per cent in the United States. Countries clipping twenty percentage points off their top rate between 1986 and 1990 included Britain (to 40 per cent), Japan (to 50 per cent), and Norway (to 20 per cent).

3. The squeezing of tax bands. Thus far it has been seen that the failure of successive Governments to index increases in basic tax allowances to increases in inflation resulted in a greater slice of employees' money incomes being exposed to income tax. Then it was shown that the abolition of the low 25 per cent rate increased the personal tax rate initially applied to taxable incomes. In themselves these constituted punishing impositions on those earning very ordinary incomes: they hit the low-paid hardest.

However, these effects were minor compared with the additional burden imposed on taxpayers by the squeezing of tax bands over the past decade. Tax codes are usually defined as progressive where the rates levied on incomes rise in step with increases in those incomes. On the surface, such systems of graduated income tax appear both reasonable and fair: as income rises, each additional band is assessed to tax at progressively higher rates. In the Irish case, however, successive Governments have added their own innovatory twist to the graduated income tax system. Throughout the period the system remained highly progressive—but only at relatively modest levels of income. Once ensnared in the income tax net, taxpayers found themselves subjected to rapidly increasing rates for relatively small additions to their incomes. As a result, even those on fairly modest incomes found themselves paying income tax at the top rate.

Since single people were restricted to half the basic tax allowances and half the width of the tax bands available to married couples, whether or not both spouses were working, they have been the main victims of the tax code's narrowly defined progressiveness. The principal agent of their financial distress has been the failure to widen tax bands in line with inflation and the pace of increase in money incomes.

In 1980/81 a single taxpayer had to earn a taxable income (gross income less all relevant allowances) of more than £5,000 before becoming liable to income tax at rates above the standard rate of 35 per cent. By 1991/92 a single taxpayer had to earn a taxable income in excess of £6,700 before being liable at a rate above the standard rate of 29 per cent. Thus the threshold for exposure to income tax at rates above the standard rate had risen only 34 per cent over an eleven-year period in which consumer price inflation topped 130 per cent. Put another way, the broadening of these tax bands lagged behind inflation by almost 100 per cent between 1980/81 and 1991/92.

The failure of tax bands to broaden in line with changes in money values pushed single taxpayers into progressively higher tax brackets even when their real incomes were not changing to any marked extent. Moreover, the ascent through the higher tax rates was particularly steep and swift for single taxpayers: in 1991/92, once taxable income exceeded £6,700, the single person's rate of tax increased from 29 to 48 per cent. Exposure to the top rate of income tax followed quickly. In 1980/81 a single person could earn £9,000 of taxable income before becoming liable to the then top rate of 60 per cent. By 1985/86 this threshold had *fallen*, even in current money terms, to £7,300. While tax bands were widened in succeeding years, even in 1991/92, once a single person's taxable income rises over £9,800 he or she is liable to tax at the top rate of 52 per cent on any additional earnings. Thus, over an eleven-year period during which average consumer prices have risen by 130.5 per cent, the amount of taxable income a single person has to earn before facing income tax at the top rate has risen by just 8.9 per cent.

Over this period, married couples at least enjoyed the consolation of qualifying for two sets of single income tax allowances and two sets of single tax bands at each tax rate, irrespective of whether one or both spouses were earning incomes. Nevertheless, the amount of taxable income that a married couple could earn before being assessed at rates above the standard rate increased by only 34 per cent, from £10,000 in 1980/81 to £13,400 in 1991/92. Again, over this eleven-year period the amount of taxable income a married couple could earn before finding themselves liable to tax at the top rate increased by just 8.9 per cent, from £18,000 in 1980/81 to £19,600 in 1991/92.

The corset of narrow tax bands squeezed the real purchasing power of all taxpayers—single and married—over the past decade.

4. The imposition of new taxes on income. The direct taxation of personal incomes over the past decade did not stop at income tax proper. Since 1980, taxes on gross income other than income tax were raised, and new taxes on income were imposed; these added significantly to the overall weight of the personal tax burden.

In 1980/81 employees on full-rate PRSI faced health contributions of 1 per cent and social insurance contributions of 3.5 per cent on their gross incomes in addition to income tax itself. While these contributions were subject to income ceilings, over the course of the decade those ceilings were adjusted upwards each year by amounts sufficient to ensure that they remained chargeable on the total incomes of average employees. The rates too were increased: from a combined rate of 4.5 per cent in 1980/81, social insurance and health contributions had increased to 6.75 per cent by 1991/92. In addition, the ceiling on the 1.25 per cent health contribution was abolished altogether in the 1991 budget, so that the health contribution became a charge on *all* income. Thus, while the Government announced that the top rate of income tax proper was being reduced from 53 to 52 per cent, the removal of the ceiling on health contributions meant in effect that the top tax rate had been increased from 53 to 53.25 per cent.

New taxes on income were also introduced. A youth employment levy of 1 per cent of all gross income was imposed in 1982/83. (The name was later changed to employment and training levy, but the rate remained the same, at 1 per cent.) When this is added onto the top rate of income tax, at 52 per cen, and the 1.25 per cent health contribution rate, the real top rate of tax for 1991/92 rises to 54.25 per cent. A further 1 per cent income levy was introduced in 1983/84, but this was discontinued in 1986/87.

Aggregating all these changes, for the average private-sector employee the hidden taxes on income have risen from 4.5 per cent in 1980/81 to 7.75 per cent of all gross income earned by 1991/92. These income taxes by another name are payable in addition to income tax proper.

These four forces, working in concert, were responsible for increasing the weight of the personal tax burden over the past decade. Sub-indexation of tax allowances exposed a larger slice of income to taxes; the abolition of the low (25 per cent) rate caused taxable income to be taxed at a very high initial rate; the compression of the tax bands, again due to sub-indexation, pushed taxpayers towards the top rate of income tax with increasing speed; and, on top of all these developments, new methods of taxing incomes directly were devised and implemented during the decade. The consequent increase in the weight of the national tax burden imposed on personal incomes was shown in table 11. Yet it was not only personal incomes that were called upon to shoulder a heftier burden of direct taxes: while employees felt the impact of rising PRSI charges throughout the 1980s, employers' contributions also increased sharply. Since 1980 the ceilings on employers' contributions have been raised progressively, while their contribution rates have increased over the period from 9.8 per cent of employees' gross pay to 12.2 per cent.

It is perhaps the final irony of the Irish tax code that business pays far more to the Government in payroll taxes on its employees' incomes than it contributes in corporation taxes levied on its own income.

THE TAX WEDGE

The sub-indexation of tax allowances and the compression of tax bands outlined in the previous chapter caused startling results. Increasing numbers of income tax payers were propelled into the higher brackets and found themselves paying tax at rates above the standard rate. This 'bracket creep' was effected through the use of inflation as a hidden instrument of taxation.

In 1973/74 just one in every hundred taxpayers paid any tax at rates above the standard rate;[1] by 1977 this proportion of surtax payers had risen to eight in every hundred. The numbers paying income tax at rates above the standard rate increased rapidly during the 1980s; by 1982/83 fifteen in every hundred taxpayers paid some tax at the higher marginal rates, and this proportion peaked in 1987/88 when 44 out of every hundred found themselves exposed to income tax at rates of 48 per cent and above. Even the concessions introduced in the three succeeding budgets only managed to reduce the proportion exposed to rates of 48 per cent and above to thirty-seven in every hundred taxpayers.[2] Thus, in the space of just seventeen years the proportion of taxpayers liable to tax at rates above the standard rate had risen from one in a hundred to more than one in three.

As well as being financially unpleasant for many taxpayers, the speed and severity of the rise in personal and payroll taxes also disturbed the workings of the labour market. For the increasing weight of the personal tax burden gave rise to an ever-widening personal tax 'wedge'. This is the gap between what it costs an employer to hire an employee and what that employee takes home in after-tax income; it consists of all income taxes levied on employee income and all payroll taxes levied on employers.

Through the imposition of indirect taxes on the prices of goods in the shops, an indirect tax wedge is created by the Government between what it costs business to produce those goods and the capacity of consumers to purchase them with their earnings. The personal tax wedge is thus superimposed on an existing indirect tax wedge.

Both the direct and indirect tax wedges cause distortions in labour markets, creating a gap between production wages and consumption wages. In this chapter attention will be directed primarily at the personal, or direct, tax wedge.

The very existence of a personal tax wedge means that the payroll cost of an employee as financed by an employer differs from the net after-tax pay actually received by that employee. Thus, employers and employees are faced with different sets of cost and income schedules when they come to make their respective decisions about hiring and working. In such circumstances there is no set of common market prices for labour that can equate labour supply to labour demand. The market demand schedule for labour is based on labour prices, including payroll costs; the market supply schedule for labour is based on the net income after taxes available to employees. Where the personal tax wedge is significant, distortions, discontinuities and inflexibility in the labour market will inevitably result. In consequence, labour resources in the economy are likely to be underutilised.

As taxes rose sharply in the early 1980s, attention was directed by the National Economic and Social Council towards the existence of a large personal tax wedge. In a paper published early in 1984 the NESC noted: 'These increases [in taxes], together with employers' contributions to the social insurance fund, have led to a widening of the gap between the take-home pay of an employee and the cost of employing to the employer.'[3]

Three years later, examining the relationship between the cost of labour to employers and the disposable income of average employees over the years 1977 to 1987, the NESC stated that the data 'points to the existence of a substantial "wedge" between the measures of wages which are of principal relevance from the respective viewpoints of employers and employees and also indicates that this "wedge" has grown rapidly in recent years. Notwithstanding the absence of conclusive empirical research on this question, it must be accounted unlikely that the patterns described . . . have evolved without seriously impacting on the labour market.'[4]

A more forthright approach was adopted by the OECD 1987/88 economic survey of Ireland. Ireland's poor record in employment creation could not be attributed solely to weak levels of demand or to restrictive fiscal policies, or to labour market inflexibility, the OECD said. Four other factors inhibited the creation of jobs in Ireland in the years to 1986. These were:

+The weakening of international competitiveness after entry into the EMS;

2—A substantial increase in taxes, which created a very large tax wedge between the after-tax wage of an average employee and the cost of hiring the employee;

—Social welfare transfers that in many cases have weakened work incentives;

4An industrial policy that has distorted relative factor prices in favour of capital and against labour and made it tax-inefficient for international companies to increase employment in Ireland.

On the basis of Ireland's policy experience, the OECD concluded: 'Over the seven years 1979–86, real labour costs have risen by about 20%. But because of higher income and indirect taxes, employees did not enjoy higher real incomes—on the contrary, real after-tax wages have fallen by over 10%. Marginal tax rates have been extremely high for a number of years: 65.5% for a single worker earning the average wage; 55.5% if he is married with two children and his wife has a [lower-paid] job. Such marginal tax rates are among the highest in the OECD area. At the same time, marginal tax rates on capital have been very low or even negative. A recent OECD study that compared the situations prevailing in different OECD countries found that no other OECD country had a tax system as biased against the use of labour as the Irish.'[5]

The OECD returned to the offensive in its 1988/89 economic survey of Ireland. Pointing out that unemployment in Ireland had risen faster during the 1980s than in any OECD country other than Spain, it noted, 'Behind Ireland's high increase in unemployment during the period of severe policy-induced demand restraint are rigidities in the labour market. These rigidities prevent increases in labour demand through real wage adjustment in response to the increase in unemployment'; and among the major causes of rigidities identified was the growing size of the tax wedge in Ireland, due to a 'continued increase in real labour costs ("real product wages") despite the decline in real take-home pay per employee ("real consumption wage"). Because of increasing direct and indirect taxes, real after-tax wages of the average employee fell by 15% between 1979 and 1983, while real labour costs to firms rose by 12%. This "tax wedge" between the real consumption wage and the real product wage has since widened by another eight percentage points.'[6]

In advocating the use of a competitive framework for analysing developments in the labour market, Patrick Geary has also drawn attention to the detrimental effects of the total tax wedge on the behaviour of the labour market. In a recent paper for the National Economic and Social Council, Geary has written:

> Viewed from the employer (or demand) side and the employee (or supply) side, the real wage has different meanings. When the operation of the tax and social welfare codes are taken into account, the difference grows. Employers' PRSI is an employment tax. The gross wage paid by the employer is thus greater than the wage received by the employee even if the latter paid no taxes. Given both employee's PRSI and income tax, the difference between the gross wage paid by the employer and the take-home pay of the employee widens substantially. When the indirect tax content (VAT, excise tax etc) of the Consumer Price Index is added, the gap is even wider. The sum of all these taxes, including PRSI, has become known as the "tax wedge"; evidence of its growth in Ireland is documented in NESC Report 83. The point to be emphasised is that by having a framework within which to consider a concept like the real wage, it becomes apparent that it is multi-faceted and that some of the facets are the result of government policies and are subject to change through changes in these policies.[7]

For much of the last decade the tax wedge expanded. This widening did not occur as the result of a conscious, deliberate policy on the part of any Government to increase the distance between what employers pay and what employees receive: rather, it was the result of piecemeal changes—and the absence of changes—in budgetary policy over the years. In part, its growth reflected the unintended side-effects of other policies. Thus, when Governments belatedly addressed the over-stretched public finance position, initially they sought to close the gap between revenue and spending by raising tax yields. They did not set out deliberately to expand the tax wedge; but if it expanded by a process of neglect, this betrays even more fundamental flaws in the conduct of Government economic policy during those years. Most centrally, it indicates laxity and incoherence in the formulation of policy. Attempts were made to reduce borrowing by raising tax yields without consideration of the distorting effects such tax increases would have on the labour market. It was only as the links between budgetary policy and labour market policy were realised—and acted upon— that the wedge began to contract once again towards the end of the decade.

Table 13

The tax wedge and its impact for single people earning the average industrial wage

Tax year	1980/81	1981/82	1982/83	1983/84	1984/85	1985/86	1986/87	1987/88	1988/89	1989/90	1990/91
1. Gross annual income (£)	5,002.40	5,837.00	6,587.88	7,360.60	8,257.08	8,915.40	9,580.48	10,069.28	10,546.64	10,970.96	11,302.20
2. Total employee deductions (£)	1,345.69	1,619.96	1,895.74	2,386.73	2,808.84	3,114.92	3,272.89	3,569.34	3,633.47	3,653.03	3,625.20
3. Employee after-tax income (£)	3,656.71	4,217.04	4,692.14	4,973.87	5,448.24	5,800.48	6,307.59	6,499.94	6,913.17	7,317.93	7,676.50
4. Direct cost of employee to employer (including PRSI) (£)	5,492.64	6,435.29	7,352.73	8,215.17	9,256.19	10,003.08	10,761.75	11,310.82	11,854.42	12,309.42	12,681.07
5. Tax wedge (4–3) (£)	1,835.93	2,218.25	2,660.59	3,241.30	3,807.95	4,202.60	4,454.16	4,810.88	4,941.25	4,991.49	5,004.57
6. Tax wedge as percentage of total labour cost to employer (5 as percentage of 4)	33.4	34.5	36.2	39.5	41.1	42.0	41.4	42.5	41.7	40.6	39.5
7. Employee's take-home pay as percentage of cost to employer (3 as percentage of 4)	66.6	65.5	63.8	60.5	58.9	58.0	58.6	57.5	58.3	59.4	60.5
8. Employee's effective personal tax rate (2 as percentage of 1)	26.9	27.8	28.8	32.4	34.0	34.9	34.2	35.4	34.5	33.3	32.1
9. Employee's marginal tax rate on additional earnings (%)	39.5	39.75	52.5	53.5	53.5	56.5	55.5	55.75	55.75	55.75	55.75
10. Cost to employer of an extra £1 in net pay to employee (£)	1.82	1.83	2.34	2.39	2.40	2.58	2.53	2.55	2.55	2.55	2.54

* Average income for 1990 is taken as that obtaining in June 1990.

41

The mechanics of the increasing tax wedge are explored in the four tables that follow. In all cases the method adopted is to apply the tax structures obtaining for each of the fiscal years 1980/81 to 1990/91, as shown in table 12, to the income data surveyed in tables 5 and 7. This allows the calculation of the taxes and other deductions from employee pay and the cost of employment to the employer for each of the years reviewed. It is then possible to track the manner in which the personal tax wedge evolved over the course of a decade.

Table 13 attempts to estimate the size of the tax wedge for single people earning the average industrial wage in manufacturing industry, and for their employers, over the years 1980 to 1990. Line 1 shows gross annual income for *all* (not only male) industrial workers in manufacturing industry. These figures are the annualised totals of the weekly average earnings shown in column 1 of table 5. Line 2 shows the total annual deductions from the average industrial worker's gross pay. These deductions include not only income tax but social insurance and health contributions, the 1 per cent youth employment levy (now the employment and training levy), and the 1 per cent income levy in the years in which the latter was imposed. These deductions are calculated on taxable income after allowance has been made for the appropriate standard tax allowances. In the case of an unmarried taxpayer these include the single tax allowance together with the PAYE and PRSI allowances available to most employees. Full-rate PRSI contributions have been charged as deductions. Line 3 shows the average single employee's income after tax and other deductions, and represents the subtraction of line 2 from line 1. Line 4 shows the direct cost to the employer of hiring an average industrial worker. It includes not only the employee's income but the employer's PRSI contributions paid on the employee's behalf. Line 5 shows the tax wedge; this is the difference between what it costs the employer to hire the average industrial worker and what that worker takes home as net income. Arithmetically, it represents line 4 less line 3.

Lines 6 to 10 of table 13 represent a number of different ways of looking at the tax wedge. Since they are expressed as proportions in all but one of the cases, they are independent of the underlying money values on which they are calculated, and year-to-year comparisons are thus possible. Line 6 shows that the tax wedge separating what employees received from what employers paid was high for single workers even at the beginning of the last decade. In 1980/81 the tax wedge was equivalent to

33.4 per cent of what it cost an employer to hire an average single industrial employee. This grew larger as the decade progressed; by 1987/88 it constituted 42.5 per cent of an employer's direct costs in hiring an average single worker. While it subsequently diminished somewhat, it still stood at 39.5 per cent in the tax year 1990/91. Line 6 thus represents the tax wedge as seen from the employer's side of the wage contract.

Line 7 of the table represents the tax wedge seen from the employee's perspective. In 1980/81 the average single employee took home only two-thirds of what the employer paid in direct labour costs; by 1987/88 employees were taking home only 57.5 per cent of that amount. Even as late as 1990/91 single employees earning the average industrial wage were taking home only three-fifths of what it cost directly to employ them. Line 8 shows the average employee's effective personal tax rate, the proportion of a single person's average earnings taken in the form of income tax and related deductions. As can be seen, the effective direct tax burden on the average earnings of single people rose from 26.9 per cent in 1980/81 to a peak of 35.4 per cent in 1987/88. By 1990/91, the average single industrial employee was still losing almost one-third of his or her income through income tax and other direct deductions from income.

The effective tax rate shows the burden of tax on all earnings. The marginal tax rate, as shown in line 9, indicates the amount of tax charged on any *additional* earnings. For the average single industrial employee, marginal income tax rates are extraordinarily high; they have risen from less than 40 per cent in 1980/81 to reach a peak of 56.5 per cent in 1985/86, and have remained on a plateau around that level ever since.

For single people on average industrial earnings, marginal rates have *not* been reduced in recent budgets. On their earnings, such single people have been trapped on the middle tax rate, facing a marginal rate of 48 per cent. While both the top and bottom rates have been cut in recent budgets, the middle rate has been left untouched at 48 per cent. When PRSI, health contributions and levies are added to the marginal rate, the effective marginal tax rate on additional earnings facing single people on average industrial earnings remained at 55.75 per cent in the 1991/92 tax year.

Line 10 in table 13 can be regarded as a set of summary statistics that present all the difficulties inherent in the tax wedge in a condensed form. In 1980/81 it cost an employer £1.82 to provide a single employee on average industrial earnings with a net increase of £1 in after-tax income; by 1985/86 the cost to the employer of providing that £1 increase had risen to £2.58. Even with the tax cuts introduced from 1988 onwards, an employer seeking to award a £1 increase in after-tax income to a single employee on average industrial earnings faced a bill of more than £2.50 in 1990/91.

Table 14 examines the impact of the tax wedge on the income of a household consisting of two adults and two children where one spouse is working and earning the average industrial wage for the years 1980 to 1990. The method is the same as that adopted in table 13.

For those on average earnings, married households where one spouse was working were levied with lower effective direct tax rates and faced smaller tax wedges throughout the 1980s than households consisting of single people. In 1980/81 a single person on average earnings lost 26.9 per cent of his or her gross income in direct taxes and other deductions; that year the effective direct tax rate borne by a married couple with two children where one spouse was earning the average industrial wage was 14.4 per cent. The married couple were thus charged only half the effective tax rate levied on a single person with a similar income.

Following the Supreme Court's decision in the Murphy case, in the 1980 budget the Minister for Finance set the tax bands and tax allowances available to married couples at twice the levels prevailing for single people, even where only one spouse was working. More than any other factor, this accounted for the much lower direct tax burden imposed on married couples than on single people at the beginning of the last decade. Thus, in the tax year 1980/81 a married couple with two children where one spouse was at work and receiving average industrial earnings lost just one-seventh of its income in income taxes and other deductions. The marginal deductions rate facing the employed spouse on any additional earnings was just 29.5 per cent, comprising a marginal income tax rate of 25 per cent and social insurance and health contributions of 4.5 per cent. The tax wedge was equivalent to 22 per cent of the cost to the employer of hiring a married person in these circumstances. This left the employee taking home 78 per cent of the production wage.

But while married couples were taxed with a much lighter touch than single people at the beginning of the decade, their effective tax burdens rose much more rapidly than those of single people as the decade progressed. The withdrawal of tax allowances for children in 1986/87 exposed more of their earnings

Table 14

The tax wedge and its impact on a household of two adults and two children, one spouse earning average industrial wage, 1980–90

Tax year	1980/81	1981/82	1982/83	1983/84	1984/85	1985/86	1986/87	1987/88	1988/89	1989/90	1990/91
1. Gross annual income (£)	5,002.40	5,837.00	6,587.88	7,360.60	8,257.08	8,915.40	9,580.40	10,069.28	10,546.64	10,970.96	11,302.20*
2. Total employee deductions (£)	720.70	993.21	1,195.65	1,606.77	1,951.73	2,168.10	2,326.61	2,559.52	2,693.58	2,701.44	2,710.78
3. Employee after-tax income (£)	4,281.70	4,843.79	5,392.23	5,753.83	6,305.35	6,747.30	7,253.87	7,509.76	7,853.06	8,269.52	8,591.42
4. Direct cost of employee to employer (including PRSI) (£)	5,492.64	6,435.29	7,352.73	8,215.17	9,256.19	10,003.08	10,761.75	11,310.82	11,854.12	12,309.42	12,681.07
5. Tax wedge (4–3) (£)	1,210.94	1,591.15	1,960.50	2,461.34	2,950.84	3,255.78	3,507.88	3,801.06	4,001.36	4,039.90	4,089.65
6. Tax wedge as percentage of total labour cost to employer (5 as percentage of 4)	22.0	24.7	26.7	30.0	31.9	32.5	32.6	33.6	33.8	32.8	32.3
7. Employee's take-home pay as percentage of cost to employer (3 as percentage of 4)	78.0	75.3	73.3	70.0	68.1	67.5	67.4	66.4	66.2	67.2	67.7
8. Employee's effective personal tax rate (2 as percentage of 1)	14.4	17.0	18.1	21.8	23.6	24.3	24.3	25.4	25.5	24.6	24.0
9. Employee's marginal tax rate on additional earnings (%)	29.5	39.75	42.5	43.5	43.5	43.5	42.5	42.75	42.75	39.75	37.75
10. Cost to employer of an extra £1 in net pay to employee (£)	1.56	1.83	1.94	1.98	1.98	1.99	1.95	1.97	1.97	1.86	1.80

* Average income for 1990 is taken as that obtaining in June 1990.

to tax. The effective rates at which they paid tax increased sharply with the cancellation of the 25 per cent income tax band in 1984/85 and with the exposure of all the increase in their nominal incomes to employees' PRSI and health contributions. As a result, the effective income taxes levied on a married couple where one spouse was working and being paid average industrial earnings rose from 14.4 per cent of gross earnings in 1980/81 to a peak of 25.5 per cent of gross earnings by 1988/89. Thus the effective income tax rate of couples in these circumstances rose by eleven percentage points within the course of the 1980s. There has been a correspondingly sharp increase in the marginal income tax rates facing such one-earner couples; marginal direct tax rates on additional earnings have risen from 29.5 per cent in 1980/81 to 36.75 per cent in 1991/92.

The tax wedge separating an employer's direct labour costs and the after-tax income of a married person earning the average industrial wage has also widened sharply over the past decade. In 1980/81 the tax wedge constituted 22 per cent of the employer's direct labour costs; by 1988/89 this had widened to 33.8 per cent of direct employment costs, as viewed from the perspective of employers. From the married employee's viewpoint the proportion of total labour cost taken home in the form of net income diminished from 78 per cent in 1980/81 to just 67.7 per cent in 1990/91.

For employees on average industrial earnings, the experience of the past decade can be summarised thus. Firstly, in the case of all such employees, married and single, effective tax rates have risen sharply in the course of the decade. Effective tax rates peaked in 1987 and 1988, before declining somewhat thereafter. Notwithstanding the fall in direct personal taxes at the end of the decade, effective tax rates on personal incomes remained very much higher in 1990 than in 1980.

Secondly, during the 1980s effective tax rates rose more rapidly for married households where one spouse was working than for single households. In part this reflects the fact that the effective tax rates borne by single people were very high at the beginning of the decade; it also mirrors the fact that, having started the decade armed with double tax allowances and tax bands, married couples saw their advantages clipped back by the abolition of the 25 per cent income tax band, by the discontinuance of tax allowances for children, and by the increasing weight of PRSI and other deductions levied on gross income.

Table 15

The tax wedge and its impact on single people earning average non-agricultural income, 1980–90

Tax Year	1980/81	1981/82	1982/83	1983/84	1984/85	1985/86	1986/87	1987/88	1988/89	1989/90
1. Gross annual income (£)	6,143.25	7,218.96	8,213.14	9,207.32	10,172.73	10,969.25	11,538.61	12,185.85	12,851.24	13,628.89
2. Total employee deductions (£)	1,796.33	2,169.68	2,748.99	3,461.84	3,982.38	4,381.34	4,464.91	4,919.31	5,029.81	5,220.26
3. Employee after-tax income (£)	4,346.92	5,049.28	5,464.15	5,745.48	6,190.35	6,587.91	7,073.70	7,266.54	7,821.43	8,408.63
4. Direct cost of employee to employer (including PRSI) (£)	6,745.29	7,958.90	9,166.69	10,276.29	11,403.63	12,307.50	12,961.32	13,688.37	14,444.79	15,291.61
5. Tax wedge (4–3) (£)	2,398.37	2,909.62	3,702.54	4,530.81	5,213.28	5,719.59	5,887.62	6,421.83	6,623.36	6,882.98
6. Tax wedge as percentage of cost to employer (5 as percentage of 4)	35.6	36.6	40.4	44.1	45.7	46.5	45.4	46.9	45.9	45.0
7. Employee's take-home pay as percentage of cost to employer (3 as percentage of 4)	64.4	63.4	59.6	55.9	54.3	53.5	54.6	53.1	54.1	55.0
8. Employee's effective personal tax rate (2 as percentage of 1)	29.2	30.1	33.5	37.6	39.1	39.9	38.7	40.4	39.1	38.3
9. Employee's marginal tax rate on additional earnings	39.5	49.75	52.5	63.5	63.5	68.5	65.5	65.75	65.75	63.75
10. Cost to employer of an extra £1 in net pay to employee (£)	1.82	2.20	2.34	3.06	3.07	3.58	3.25	3.28	3.28	3.09

Thirdly, reflecting both the increased weight of the personal tax burden and the rising cost of employers' PRSI contributions, the tax wedge widened considerably, whether judged from the standpoint of employers or employees. Thus the gap between consumption wages (what employees have to spend) and production wages (what employers have to pay) widened for most of the decade, although it narrowed somewhat from the point of its greatest width in the final years of the 1980s.

Fourthly, the marginal tax rates facing all employees—the deductions levied on any additional earnings—have risen very steeply, and more sharply for spouses in single-income married households than for single people. Because single people on average industrial earnings are locked into the middle tax rate of 48 per cent, and since that rate has been left unchanged, their marginal tax rates have *not* declined in recent years.

Thus far, the argument has been conducted solely in terms of average industrial earnings for those at work in manufacturing industry. This may or may not constitute an accurate reflection of average employee earnings throughout the economy; we do not know, since no comprehensive data on Irish earnings exists. However, from the data collated in tables 5 and 7, there is an amount of evidence that suggests that the average industrial earnings of all those at work in industry—the figures used so far— understate the actual level of earnings amongst non-agricultural employees throughout the economy.

Tables 15 and 16 examine the impact on the tax wedge at higher levels of income, both for single people and for married couples where only one spouse is working. The income data in these tables is derived from table 7, and similar caveats apply. The income data in tables 15 and 16 can be read in two ways. Firstly, they can be seen as a more accurate reflection of average non-agricultural employee remuneration in the economy, allowing for some overstatement because of the treatment of employers' pension contributions. Alternatively, they can be seen simply as how the tax wedge widens as income levels rise above the average level of earnings in manufacturing industry.

As can be seen from table 15, the effective direct tax rate borne by single people with average gross earnings increased very sharply, from 29.2 per cent of gross pay in 1980/81 to 39.1 per cent in 1984/85, an increase of ten percentage points. Having scaled that peak, effective tax rates remained on a plateau almost for the rest of the decade. The stiff deductions made from these incomes when earned by single people, combined with the rising

Table 16

The tax wedge and its impact on a household of two adults and two children, one spouse earning average non-agricultural income, 1980–90

Tax Year	1980/81	1981/82	1982/83	1983/84	1984/85	1985/86	1986/87	1987/88	1988/89	1989/90
1. Gross annual income (£)	6,143.25	7,218.96	8,213.14	9,207.32	10,172.73	10,969.25	11,538.61	12,185.85	12,851.24	13,628.89
2. Total employee deductions (£)	1,169.58	1,542.54	1,886.38	2,410.07	2,785.04	3,061.53	3,158.81	3,464.35	3,678.80	3,757.96
3. Employee after-tax income (£)	4,973.67	5,676.42	6,326.76	6,797.25	7,387.69	7,907.72	8,379.80	8,721.50	9,172.44	9,870.93
4. Direct cost of employee to employer (including PRSI) (£)	6,745.29	7,958.90	9,166.69	10,276.29	11,403.63	12,307.50	12,961.32	13,688.37	14,444.79	15,291.62
5. Tax wedge (4–3) (£)	1,771.62	2,282.48	2,839.93	3,479.04	4,015.94	4,399.78	4,581.52	4,966.87	5,272.35	5,420.69
6. Tax wedge as percentage of total labour cost to employer (5 as percentage of 4)	26.3	28.7	31.0	33.9	35.2	35.7	35.3	36.3	36.5	35.4
7. Employee's take-home pay as percentage of cost to employer (3 as percentage of 4)	73.7	71.3	69.0	66.1	64.8	64.3	64.7	63.7	63.5	64.6
8. Employee's effective personal tax rate (2 as percentage of 1)	19.0	21.4	23.0	26.2	27.4	27.9	27.4	28.4	28.6	27.6
9. Employee's marginal tax rate on additional earnings (%)	39.5	39.75	42.5	42.5	43.5	43.5	42.5	42.75	42.75	39.75
10. Cost to employer of an extra £1 in net pay to employee (£)	1.82	1.83	1.94	1.94	1.98	1.99	1.95	1.97	1.97	1.86

cost of PRSI contributions exacted from their employers, drove a deep tax wedge between such employees' after-tax incomes and the direct labour costs borne by their employers.

In 1980/81 the gap between the consumption wage earned by single employees and the production wage paid by their employers came to 35.6 per cent of the employers' direct labour costs. This wedge widened quickly in the first half of the decade. On average, throughout the second half of the decade the personal tax wedge exceeded 45 per cent of the employer's cost of financing a job.

The marginal tax rates faced by such single employees on additional earnings rose even more dramatically during the decade. At the beginning of the 1980s those single people earning average gross non-agricultural incomes faced deductions of 39.5 per cent on any additional earnings. By 1985/86 the marginal direct tax rates faced had escalated to 68.5 per cent on extra pay. Some correction has been effected in the very recent past. By 1991/92 the marginal tax rates on the additional earnings of such single people have been reduced to 59.75 per cent.

The combined effect of these forces is reflected in what it cost an employer to grant such employees a net pay increase of £1. The cost of such an increase—including the additional employers' PRSI—rose from £1.82 in 1980/81 to a peak of £3.58 in 1985/86, before declining to £3.09 in 1989/90.

The impact of the tax wedge on a married couple, one of whom is working and earning average gross non-agricultural pay, is examined in table 16. While the effects are less dramatic than in the case of the single person, this should not be allowed to obscure the fact that the width of the tax wedge, the effective personal tax rate and the marginal tax rate confronted have all grown significantly in the course of the last decade. For such a couple, the effective income taxes taken from gross income have risen by almost nine percentage points, from 19 per cent of gross income in 1980/81 to 27.6 per cent in 1989/90. In similar fashion, the size of the tax wedge, viewed from the employer's standpoint, has risen from 26.3 per cent of total direct labour costs in 1980/81 to 35.4 per cent in 1989/90; this has left the working spouse taking home 64.6 per cent of what it costs the employer to hire him or her in 1989/90, compared with 73.7 per cent in the first year of the decade. In this instance, marginal tax rates have *not* risen in the course of the decade. The rise in PRSI contributions and income levies has been offset by the reduction in the standard tax rate.

Thus, to the conclusions adduced earlier one additional finding can be added. Relatively small increases in employee income—shown here as the difference between the average earnings of all industrial workers in manufacturing industry and average non-agricultural incomes—have resulted over the last decade in significant increases in effective tax rates, marginal tax rates, and the width of the tax wedge. This conclusion derives from the compressed nature of the tax code and the steep progressiveness in direct tax rates at relatively low levels of income.

To what extent does all this matter? Do economic agents—whether they are employers or employees, men or women, married or single—actually change their behaviour as a result of changes in taxes or changes in their incomes engineered by changes in taxes?

The labour market framework advocated by Geary can be used to explore the likely outcomes. It places emphasis on three factors:

(1) the decisions of employers about how many people to hire, what type of people to hire and how many hours should be worked, i.e. on the determinants of the demand for labour;

(2) the decisions of individuals about whether or not to participate in the labour force and, if in employment, about how many hours to work should a choice be offered, i.e. on the determinants of the supply of labour;

(3) the interactions of the decisions of the demanders and suppliers of labour, which determine the actual levels of employment, earnings, fringe benefits and other conditions observed in the economy.[7]

The extensive discussion of the relevant empirical literature, both Irish and international, in Geary's paper obviates the need for its repetition here. It is worth, however, making the following selective points.

Firstly, the very existence of a tax wedge causes dislocation in the functioning of the labour market. As taxes drive a wedge between the consumption wages earned by employees and production wages as paid by employers, employees and employers are talking a different language when it comes to discussing wages. As a result, the market mechanism's most valuable characteristic, its communicative ability manifested through price signalling, is distorted. Employees and employers are each responding to different sets of price signals where a tax wedge exists; as the width of this wedge increases, market communication becomes progressively more distorted, and the capacity of the market mechanism to reconcile the wishes of job seekers and job providers is debilitated. A large tax wedge makes it difficult for potential employers and potential employees to talk the same language about jobs.

Secondly, on *a priori* grounds, an increase in the cost of labour to employers would be expected to reduce the demand for labour. This is borne out by empirical findings, both at home and abroad. In the Irish case, Geary found that in most studies a 1 per cent increase in labour costs was associated with a decline of between 0.6 and 1 per cent in employment.

Thirdly, other things being equal, the response of the labour supply to a change in real wages is consistent only in the ambiguity of the results yielded. In response to an increase in real wages, hours worked may increase, decrease, or remain the same, depending on the circumstances and the manner in which the real wage increase was engineered. The actual observed outcome will depend on the relative strengths of 'income' and 'substitution' effects.

However, the tax wedge has been found to cause unemployment in Ireland, both directly and through the wage pressures it induces. The disincentive effects of very high marginal tax rates have been accepted as important by the National Economic and Social Council in its report *A Strategy for the Nineties*. That report states:

> There are a number of reasons why reductions in MTRs are desirable. Two in particular stand out—one efficiency-based and one equity-based. The efficiency argument is that most of the incentive and disincentive effects of taxation are related to the size of marginal tax rates ... It is not at all clear that the disincentive effects of marginal tax rates on labour supply are greater for those with average earnings and above. It is likely that the greatest disincentive effects arise from the interaction of the tax and welfare system and are, therefore, relevant to those whose earnings or potential earnings are well below average male earnings in manufacturing industry.[8]

It is to the interaction of the tax and social welfare systems that we now turn.

Notes
1. National Economic and Social Council, *Economic and Social Policy, 1983: Aims and Recommendations* (report no. 75), Dublin: NESC 1984, 16.

2. Budget, 1990, presented to Dáil Éireann by Albert Reynolds TD, Minister for Finance, 31 January 1990, 35.
3. NESC, *Economic and Social Policy*, para. 1.54.
4. National Economic and Social Council, *A Strategy for Development, 1986–1990*, Dublin: NESC 1986, 84.
5. Organisation for Economic Co-operation and Development, *OECD Economic Surveys, 1987/1988: Ireland*, Paris: OECD 1987, 46–8.
6. Organisation for Economic Co-operation and Development, *OECD Economic Surveys, 1988/1989: Ireland*, Paris: OECD 1989, 42–5.
7. Patrick Geary, *The Nature and Functioning of Labour Markets* (report no. 86), Dublin: NESC 1988, 5–6.
8. National Economic and Social Council, *A Strategy for the Nineties: Economic Stability and Structural Change* (report no. 89) [draft], Dublin: NESC 1990, chap. 6.19.

THE SOCIAL WELFARE SAFETY NET

The social welfare system provides a safety net for the less well-off and the disadvantaged in Irish society. That safety net is extensive, both in the range of support provided and in the numbers of people who call upon it. In scope, social welfare benefits range from payments to the old and the ill, through family income support, to benefits provided to the unemployed. In 1989 the number of people claiming social welfare benefits stood at 715,540, while total beneficiaries—including children—numbered almost 1.3 million people.

No matter what measuring rod is used, public spending on the provision of social welfare benefits increased significantly during the 1980s. Three factors accounted for the increase in social welfare spending. First, the number of claimants on existing programmes increased; second, new social welfare programmes were introduced during the course of the decade; third, increases in benefit rates rose faster than inflation during the decade. To put it another way, the real purchasing power of social welfare benefits, taken in aggregate, increased during the 1980s.

These trends are illustrated in table 17. As can be seen, expenditure on social welfare almost tripled between 1980 and 1989, while consumer prices doubled. Public expenditure on social welfare increased from 10.0 per cent of GNP in 1980 to a peak at 14.8 per cent in 1986. Thereafter it fell back, to 13 per cent of GNP in 1989. Over the decade, however, social welfare spending increased its share of GNP by three percentage points. As a proportion of total current Government spending, social welfare increased from less than 25 per cent in 1980 to 33.2 per cent in 1989. As public expenditure was squeezed after 1987, social welfare spending increased its share of what remained.

In terms of programme allocations, the largest segment of social welfare expenditure in 1988 was earmarked for the old (30 per cent); this was followed by expenditure on payments for the unemployed (26 per cent) and for family income support (25.6 per cent); the remainder was allocated to programmes supporting the incomes of the ill, miscellaneous benefits, and the

	Table 17

Expenditure on social welfare, 1980–90

Year	Social welfare spending (£ million)	Social welfare spending as percentage of current Government expenditure	Social welfare spending as percentage of GNP	Index of social welfare spending (1980 = 100)	Consumer price index (1980 = 100)
1980	899	24.3	10.0	100.0	100.0
1981	1,192	25.0	11.0	133	120.4
1982	1,630	27.6	13.1	181	141.1
1983	1,900	30.0	14.0	211	155.8
1984	2,093	29.9	14.2	233	169.2
1985	2,298	30.2	14.6	256	178.4
1986	2,480	30.6	14.8	276	185.2
1987	2,593	31.1	14.4	288	191.0
1988	2,614	32.6	13.9	291	195.1
1989	2,663	33.2	13.0	296	203.1

Source: *Statistical Information on Social Welfare Services*, 1989, Department of Social Welfare, November 1990, table A2.

administration of the system. Thus, social welfare payments to the unemployed absorb more than a quarter of all social welfare spending and constitute the second-largest area of expenditure within the social welfare system.

Social welfare support for the unemployed takes two forms. First, those who are in employment pay social insurance contributions; as a result, on losing their jobs they are entitled to social insurance payments in the form of unemployment benefit and pay-related benefit. Since these are entitlements, they are paid irrespective of the means of the claimant. Second, for those who have not been paying social insurance contributions or whose entitlements have expired, social welfare support is available in the form of unemployment assistance. Typically, unemployment assistance claimants comprise the long-term unemployed. Those who have lost their jobs exhaust their entitlement to unemployment benefit after roughly fifteen months; they then transfer to unemployment assistance. Unlike unemployment benefit, unemployment assistance is means-tested. In both cases there are separate rates of payment for single people, for claimants with adult dependants, and for those with both adult and child dependants. These payments are not assessable for income tax.

6

Rates of unemployment benefit and unemployment assistance for different categories of claimants for the period 1980–91 are shown in table 18. In the early 1980s, increases in benefit rates announced in the budget were conventionally paid in two stages, in April and October. From 1984 onwards a single annual increase has been awarded, payable in July of each year. The unemployment assistance rates shown are those payable in urban areas to the long-term unemployed.

Table 18

Rates of unemployment benefit and unemployment assistance

	Unemployment benefit			Unemployment assistance		
Year	Personal rate (£)	Person with adult dependant (£)	Person, adult dependant, two children (£)	Personal rate (£)	Person with adult dependant (£)	Person, adult dependant, two children (£)
1980	20.45	33.70	45.60	17.00	29.25	39.85
1981	24.25	40.45	53.45	20.40	35.10	46.70
1982	31.65	52.15	68.05	26.25	45.20	59.10
1983	34.80	57.35	74.85	28.90	49.75	65.15
1984*	37.25	61.40	80.15	32.80	56.45	73.90
1985	39.50	65.10	85.10	34.95	60.15	78.75
1986	41.10	67.70	87.60	36.70	63.15	81.75
1987	42.30	69.70	90.20	37.80	65.00	84.20
1988	43.60	71.80	93.00	42.00	70.00	90.40
1989	45.00	74.00	95.80	47.00	76.00	97.00
1990	48.00	79.00	101.80	52.00	83.00	105.00
1991	50.00	83.00	107.00	55.00	88.00	112.00

* From 1984 onwards, rates of unemployment and disability benefit and of unemployment assistance were increased annually in July, and these are the rates shown for the period from 1984 onwards. For the years 1980 to 1983 the rates shown are those announced in the budget and introduced in April of each year.

Note: The means-tested rates of unemployment assistance shown are the long-term urban assistance rates, where applicable. The distinction between long-term and short-term assistance was introduced in 1984. The distinction between urban and rural assistance rates was abolished in July 1989.

Source: Department of Social Welfare.

As can be seen from table 18, a significant policy shift occurred during the 1980s. At the beginning of the decade, rates of unemployment benefit stood significantly above maximum unemployment assistance payments. The gap narrowed as the decade progressed, and by 1989 weekly rates of unemployment assistance had risen above rates of unemployment benefit for comparable households. This trend was continued in the 1991 budget.

Table 19 presents the increases that occurred both in unemployment benefit and in unemployment assistance during the 1980s in the form of index numbers, with a base of 1980 = 100. This allows a comparison to be made between rates of increase in social welfare payments to the unemployed and rates of increase in consumer prices. The table shows that Governments have honoured their commitments to keep social welfare benefits rising at a faster pace than prices.

Table 19					
Real gains in unemployment benefits, 1980–90					
	Unemployment benefit		Unemployment assistance		
Year	Personal rate	Household, two adults, two children	Personal rate	Household, two adults, two children	Consumer price index
1980	100	100	100	100	100
1981	118.6	117.2	120.0	117.2	120.4
1982	154.8	149.2	154.4	148.3	141.0
1983	170.2	164.1	170.0	163.5	155.8
1984	182.2	175.8	192.9	185.4	169.2
1985	193.2	186.6	205.6	197.6	178.4
1986	200.1	192.1	215.9	205.1	185.2
1987	206.8	197.8	222.3	211.3	191.0
1988	213.2	203.9	247.1	226.9	195.1
1989	220.0	210.1	276.5	243.4	203.1
1990	234.7	223.2	305.9	263.5	210.6*

* August
Sources: Table 17; Consumer Price Index (CSO).

Consumer prices doubled between 1980 and 1990. Unemployment benefit for a household of two adults and two children increased two-and-a-quarter times over this period, while the personal rate of unemployment benefit increased two-and-a-third times during the decade. For those on unemployment assistance the personal rate trebled between 1980 and 1990, while a household of two adults and two children benefited from an increase of 163.5 per cent in unemployment assistance during the decade. These figures again confirm the policy

Table 20

The curtailment of pay-related benefit during the 1980s

Year (April)	PRB ceiling (£)	PRB floor (£)	Relevant PRB income (£)	PRB benefit rates	Maximum weekly payments (£)	Payment limits as percentage of previous income
1980	7,000	700	6,300	Initially 40% falling to 20%	50.40	No limit
1981	8,500	1,000	7,500	Same	60.00	No limit
1982	9,500	1,250	8,250	Same	66.00	No limit
1983	11,000	1,800	9,200	25% first 141 days 20% next 234 days	46.00	80% previous income
1984	11,000	2,150	8,850	25%/20%	44.25	75% last income
1985	11,000	2,450	8,550	25%/20%	42.75	75%
1986	11,000	2,900	8,100	25%/20%	40.25	75%
1987	11,000	3,100	7,900	12% single rate	18.96	75%
1988	11,000	3,300	7,700	12%	18.50	75%
1989	11,000	3,450	7,550	12%	18.10	75%
1990	11,000	3,600	7,400	12%	17.80	75%
1991	11,000	3,750	7,250	12%	17.40	75%

Note: Method of calculating pay-related benefit: (ceiling/50–floor/50) x benefit rate. Thus in 1990: (£11,000/50 – £3,600/50) (0.12) = (£220 – £72) (0.12) = (£148) (0.12) = £17.76, rounded up to £17.80.
Source: Department of Social Welfare.

bias towards support for the long-term unemployed during the 1980s.

However, unemployment benefit is only one of the sources of income available to the newly unemployed. In 1974 pay-related benefit was introduced to cushion the initial financial impact of the loss of a job. With pay-related benefit the newly unemployed worker receives additional payments based on gross earnings in the previous tax year. (The mechanics of the benefit are explained in table 20.) Thus a newly unemployed worker who was paying social insurance contributions while at work is entitled to two forms of social welfare support on losing employment: unemployment benefit and pay-related benefit. As can be seen from table 20, pay-related benefit constituted a substantial source of income in the early 1980s for those who had just lost their jobs. Up to 1983 this benefit was paid at the rate of 40 per cent of previous relevant earnings for the first six months of unemployment; by 1982 the maximum weekly payment was set as high as £66. Moreover, no restriction was imposed to prevent the joint income from unemployment benefit and pay-related benefit exceeding previous gross earnings from employment. Some people could—and did—have a higher net income from unemployment benefit than from prior employment.

However, all that ended in 1983. Firstly, the rate at which pay-related benefit was paid for the initial period of unemployment was cut from 40 per cent of previous gross earnings to 25 per cent. Secondly, total income from unemployment benefit was restricted to 80 per cent of previous gross earnings. The following year the ceiling on income from unemployment benefits was reduced further, to 75 per cent of previous earnings. Following the introduction of these restrictions the cash income provided to the newly unemployed through pay-related benefit was severely curtailed. Maximum weekly pay-related benefit fell from £66 in 1982 to £44.25 in 1984; a further cut was introduced in 1987, when the payment rate was reduced to a single tier of 12 per cent for the first fifteen months of unemployment. These policy changes, together with the gradual erosion of the prior income on which pay-related benefit is based, led to a very sharp drop in maximum payments. In cash terms the maximum pay-related benefit fell from £50.40 in 1980 to a mere £17.40 in 1991. The scheme is now only a shadow of the original benefit.

Thus, while basic entitlements under unemployment benefit and unemployment assistance both outpaced inflation during the 1980s, the deep erosion of pay-related benefit caused the total package of payments available to the newly unemployed to lag significantly *behind* inflation during the decade. Since pay-related benefit is restricted to those on social insurance and therefore has no effect on the income of the long-term unemployed, the restrictions further tilted the balance in the welfare system towards the support of the long-term unemployed in the latter years of the decade.

Traditionally, much of the economic analysis regarding participation in the labour market has centred on the trade-off between labour and leisure. In the standard framework, if wages fell, leisure would be substituted for work and the supply of labour would contract; if wages rose, then work would become relatively more attractive and the supply of labour seeking employment would increase. In these simple textbook models, governments did not appear on the scene to any appreciable extent. Government taxes and benefits, employers' payroll taxes and the gap between production and consumption wages that resulted tended to be left out of supply and demand calculations. However, over the past twenty years the government has elbowed itself onto the centre of the labour market stage through the very sharp rise in official intervention in all industrial economies over that period. The growth in the weight of personal tax burdens and employers' payroll taxes on the one hand and the extension of the social welfare safety net on the other hand have necessitated significant amendments and additions to the traditional textbook model.

From the employees' side of the labour market, the decision to participate and to seek employment is no longer simply a matter of comparing the gross pay offered by the employer against an alternative income of zero from not working. Instead, two separate decisions are required. Firstly, the employee must calculate his or her net income after the deduction of income tax, social insurance, health contributions and other levies on gross income. Secondly, the employee must compare net after-tax income from work against the income available for being unemployed. Being without work no longer means being without an income, and the size of the income available to the unemployed depends on two crucial variables: the duration of unemployment, and family size and circumstances.

Attempts to integrate the effects of Government intervention, both through taxes and social welfare transfers, into analyses of the labour market have resulted in the calculation of *income replacement ratios*. These ratios seek to ascertain how much of previous net after-tax income is replaced by social welfare payments available to the unemployed. The result is a series of 'snapshots' of income before and after unemployment.

It must be emphasised from the outset that great care has to be taken both in calculating and interpreting these ratios, and for a number of reasons. Firstly, such calculations are heavily influenced by the scope of what is included. Where cash income only is included, such ratios will tend to *understate* the extent to which earned income is replaced by social welfare income, since non-cash benefits such as reduced local authority differential rents charged to the unemployed are excluded. Secondly, income replacement ratios are extremely sensitive both to timing and to family circumstances, since unemployment benefits vary both with the duration of unemployment and the number of those dependent on the unemployed person's income. Thirdly, in consequence, it is very difficult to define 'average' income replacement ratios; their size depends wholly on the assumptions adopted and the information included in their estimation. Care must be taken in formulating general conclusions from specific cases.

Bearing these caveats in mind, four sets of income replacement ratios, reflecting differing durations of unemployment and differing family circumstances, have been estimated in tables 21 and 22. In both of these tables, only cash income is counted; non-cash benefits are excluded. Nor is any attempt made to assess the 'transactions' costs of working: travel to and from work and the additional cost of meals taken outside the home. These tables thus reflect a comparison between the after-tax income gained from employment and the net income arising from unemployment benefits of various types.

Table 21 illustrates the case of a single person receiving average industrial earnings in manufacturing industry. Income tax and other state deductions are subtracted from gross earnings for each of the years 1980 to 1990 to yield the single person's net after-tax income from employment. This net after-tax income is then compared, in the first place, against the net income from unemployment benefits accruing to a newly unemployed single person. In this case unemployment payments consist both of unemployment benefit and pay-related benefit, the latter benefit being calculated on the newly unemployed person's earnings in the previous *completed* tax year. Income replacement ratio A then shows the proportion of a single person's previous net earnings from employment that was replaced by unemployment benefits when that single person initially became unemployed.

Table 21

Short-term and long-term income replacement ratios for single people relative to average industrial earnings in manufacturing industry, 1980–90

Year	Weekly average gross earnings (£)	Net after-tax income (£)	Short-term replacement		Long-term replacement	
			Unemployment benefits (UB plus PRB) (£)	Income replacement ratio A (%)	Unemployment assistance (£)	Income replacement ratio B (%)
1980	96.20	70.32	43.11	61.3	17.00	24.2
1981	112.25	81.10	48.81	60.2	20.40	25.2
1982	126.69	90.23	60.13	66.6	26.25	29.1
1983	141.55	95.65	53.86	56.3	28.90	30.2
1984	158.79	104.77	58.17	55.5	32.80	31.3
1985	171.45	111.55	62.64	56.2	34.95	31.3
1986	184.24	121.30	66.30	54.7	36.70	30.3
1987	193.64	125.00	55.43	44.3	37.80	30.2
1988	202.82	132.95	57.79	43.5	42.00	31.6
1989	210.98	141.08	59.96	42.5	47.00	33.3
1990	217.35*	147.63	63.70	43.1	52.00	35.2

* in June 1990

Sources: Calculated from tables 5, 17, 19. The earnings figure for 1990 relates to June 1990.

As can be seen, a very high proportion of previous net earnings was replaced by unemployment benefits for a newly unemployed single worker in the early years of the 1980s. By 1982 a single person in the initial phase of unemployment was receiving two-thirds of his or her previous net income from employment in the form of unemployment benefits, even on the relatively restrictive assumptions adopted here. This high replacement ratio for the average industrial earner reflected the extent to which basic unemployment benefit was topped up with generous pay-related benefit payments. But as restrictions were imposed on the latter from 1983 onwards, the proportion of previous earnings replaced by benefits began a long downward slide. This decline in the income replacement ratio for the newly unemployed occurred in spite of the fact that unemployment benefits themselves were overindexed for inflation each year.

By 1989 the average single industrial worker who had just lost his or her job found that unemployment benefits replaced only 42.5 per cent of previous net income. Thus, between 1982 and 1989 the income replacement ratio for such a person declined by twenty-four percentage points.

The shrinkage in the cushion of pay-related benefit can be gauged from data contained in the Department of Social Welfare's *Statistical Information on Social Welfare Services, 1989.* It points out that the number of unemployed people claiming pay-related benefit during 1989 averaged 23,349 and that the average weekly payment under the scheme came to £10.58.

Preliminary data for 1990 suggests that for the newly un-employed, the income replacement ratio increased for the first time in many years. This reflects on the one hand the slow growth in average industrial earnings and on the other hand the significant rise of 6.6 per cent in the personal rate of unemploy-ment benefit. By 1990 the short-term income replacement ratio stood at an estimated 43.1 per cent for the average industrial worker, more than eighteen percentage points lower than it had been a decade earlier. In the second place, table 21 shows the proportion of a single person's average industrial earnings that is replaced by maximum cash means-tested unemployment assistance, which is primarily aimed at the long-term unemployed. The proportion of average earnings replaced for a single person by unemployment assistance is shown as income replacement ratio B.

As can be seen, the trend in the income replacement ratio for the long-term unemployed has been in the opposite direction to that for the newly unemployed during the 1980s. At the beginning of the decade a relatively small proportion of average industrial earnings was replaced for a single person by unemployment assistance; but since the long-term unemployed cannot avail of pay-related benefit, their social welfare incomes were unaffected by the cut-backs in pay-related benefit that occurred during the 1980s. In addition, from 1988 onwards large increases were granted in each year's budget in maximum payments under unemployment assistance; as a result, in the course of the decade the proportion of net after-tax industrial earnings replaced by unemployment assistance rose by eleven percentage points, from 24.2 per cent of net earned income in 1980 to 35.2 per cent by 1990.

During the 1980s the decline in the income replacement ratio facing the newly unemployed, coupled with the increase in the ratio available to single people who have experienced long spells of unemployment, eroded much of the gap that initially existed between the two ratios. Whereas in 1980 a single person on average industrial earnings received more than three-fifths of previous earnings on being made redundant, a single person who had experienced a prolonged spell of unemployment received less than a quarter of average industrial earnings that year by way of unemployment assistance. By 1990, however, the proportion of previous net earnings replaced by the combination of unemployment benefit and pay-related benefit had declined to 43.1 per cent for a newly unemployed single person, while the income replacement ratio for a single person numbered among the long-term unemployed has risen to 35.2 per cent of average net industrial earnings in that year.

Income replacement ratios are much higher for unemployed couples with child dependants than for single people; this is shown clearly in table 22. The reason is that there are additional payments, both under unemployment benefit and unemployment assistance, for the adult and child dependants of an unemployed person. The case of a married couple with two children where the working spouse has been made redundant in the recent past is represented by income replacement ratio C in table 22. Here the unemployment benefit for both adults and two children combined with pay-related benefit provided the household with 83 per cent of its previous average net income in 1980. (It is assumed here that before being made redundant the working spouse had been receiving average industrial earnings.) By 1982 such a household's net income from social welfare

Table 22

Short-term and long-term income replacement ratios for a married couple with two children, 1980–90

Year	Gross earnings (£)	Net after-tax income (£)	Short-term replacement Unemployment benefits (UB plus PRB)(£)	Income replacement ratio C (%)	Long-term replacement Unemployment assistance (£)	Income replacement ratio D (%)
1980	96.20	82.34	68.26	82.9	39.85	47.2
1981	112.25	93.15	78.01	83.7	46.70	50.1
1982	126.69	103.70	96.53	93.1	59.10	57.0
1983	141.55	110.65	88.52	80.0	65.15	58.9
1984	158.79	121.26	90.95	75.0	73.90	60.9
1985	171.45	129.76	97.32	75.0	78.75	60.7
1986	184.24	139.50	104.63	75.0	81.75	58.6
1987	193.64	144.42	103.33	71.5	84.20	58.3
1988	202.82	151.02	107.19	71.0	90.40	59.9
1989	210.98	159.03	110.76	69.6	97.00	61.0
1990	217.35*	165.22	117.50	71.1	105.00	63.6

* in June 1990

Note: From 1983 to 1986, short-term entitlements would have been higher in the absence of the 80% and 75% rules limiting actual payments.

Source: Department of Social Welfare.

benefits had risen to 93.1 per cent of average after-tax income that year. However, the introduction of the ceiling of 80 per cent in 1983 and of 75 per cent from 1984 onwards squeezed the short-term replacement ratio downwards. By 1990 this ratio had fallen to 71.1 per cent of that year's after-tax income from employment, almost twelve percentage points below the 1980 short-term replacement ratio.

The case of a household dependent on a spouse who has been out of work for a long time is represented by income replacement ratio D. Here the household of two unemployed adults and two children have seen their social welfare incomes rise significantly as a proportion of prospective after-tax income from employment over the past decade. Unemployment assistance to such a four-person household provided 47.2 per cent of what would have been available to it from average industrial earnings after tax in 1980. With increases in unemployment assistance outpacing inflation as the decade progressed, social welfare benefits replaced a continuously higher proportion of the after-tax income that would have been provided by the average industrial job. By 1990 the maximum rates of unemployment assistance replaced 63.6 per cent of what would have been yielded in after-tax income by the average industrial job. Thus, over the space of the decade the long-term income replacement ratio for a household of two adults and two children had climbed by more than sixteen percentage points.

In conclusion, it is clear that the social welfare system does provide a significant financial safety net for those who are out of work. For single people, unemployment benefits replace between 35 and 43 per cent of the net after-tax earnings that would have been provided by an average industrial job, with the replacement ratio being higher for the newly unemployed. For families dependent on an unemployed adult, the income available from unemployment benefits constitutes an even higher proportion of the after-tax income that would have been yielded by the average job. For households of two adults and two children, unemployment benefits replace between 63 and 71 per cent of net after-tax income from the average industrial job.

Over the past decade there have been significant shifts in replacement ratios. Short-term income replacement ratios, those supporting the recently redundant, have fallen very sharply since 1980, principally because of the policy squeeze effected on income from pay-related benefit. These sharp declines in short-term income replacement ratios hold irrespective of whether the claimants are married or single. In sharp contrast, the cash benefits provided to the long-term unemployed have risen consistently and continuously as a proportion of the prospective after-tax income that would be provided by the average industrial job. Again, this holds irrespective of whether the claimants are single or married.

In stark cash terms, leaving aside all other considerations, the recently unemployed now have more reason, and the long-term unemployed less reason, to seek re-employment than they had a decade ago.

THE LOW-PAID

In previous chapters the impact of the personal tax and benefit system on those earning average incomes was assessed. It has been made clear throughout that estimates of tax burdens, tax wedges and income replacement ratios are particularly sensitive to the specific characteristics of the examples selected. Thus, while average earnings have served as the basis for calculations, the results cannot be taken as representative of the working population at large; individual financial circumstances are simply too diverse to be captured by any set of particularised examples. However, the domestic employment prospects of two specific segments of the labour force have been diminished to a significant extent by the evolution of the tax and benefit system over the past decade. Those hit hardest have been the low-paid and single people. Their positions are examined in the following two chapters.

Low pay itself makes employment unattractive. The incentives for working at low money wages have been further diminished in recent years by three factors. Firstly, effective income taxes are high at relatively low income levels. In part this reflects the fact that the initial rate of income tax is very high. As can be seen from table 23, the first rate of income tax to which taxpayers are exposed in Ireland is higher than in all industrial countries apart from Iceland. Secondly, income levies are charged on *all* gross income, no matter how low, while social insurance contributions must be paid by all employees earning more than £60 a week. Thirdly, increases in the real value of untaxed basic unemployment benefits have enhanced their attractions relative to low taxed income from employment.

From the point of view of the labour market, these three developments pose particular difficulties. The past decade has witnessed a very sharp rise in the numbers registered as unemployed; within the total out of work, the proportion of long-term unemployed has also risen significantly. At April 1990, when the number of unemployed on the 'live register' stood at 232,251, a total of 100,266 or 45 per cent of all those

Table 23

First income tax rates faced by taxpayers in OECD countries, 1990

Rank	Country	Initial income tax rate, 1990 (%)
1.	Iceland	33
2.	IRELAND	30
3.	Spain	25
4.	Turkey	25
5.	Belgium	25
6.	Britain	25
7.	New Zealand	24
8.	Denmark	22
9.	Australia	21
10.	Sweden	20
11.	Germany (Federal Republic)	19
12.	Greece	18
13.	Canada	17
14.	United States	15
15.	Netherlands	13
16.	Norway	10
17.	Japan	10
18.	Luxembourg	10
19.	Italy	10
20.	Austria	10
21.	Finland	9
22.	France	5
23.	Switzerland	1

Source: *The Public Sector: Issues for the 1990s* (OECD, Paris 1990). The data in the table pre-date the budget of 1991, which reduced the starting rate of income tax in Ireland to 29%.

7

registered had been unemployed for more than one year. Illustrating the ingrained nature of Ireland's unemployment problem, 46,656 or 21 per cent of the total had been out of work for more than three years.

Getting the long-term unemployed back to work presents very great difficulties. As the duration of unemployment lengthens, work skills—both general and specific—tend to deteriorate. Those among the long-term unemployed who have never had a job find it progressively more difficult to countenance employment as a feasible option. The long-term unemployed are not likely to command high earnings even where job opportunities do materialise; for most, the only option to being out of work is low-paid employment.

This chapter examines the interaction of the tax and benefit systems for the low-paid, viewed from the perspective of the long-term unemployed contemplating a return to work. For purposes of illustration, 'low pay' is taken as constituting half of the average earnings in manufacturing for each of the years 1980 to 1990.

Those who have experienced prolonged spells of unemployment can claim unemployment assistance. This is a means-tested benefit, but it is not subject to income tax. For a single person with no dependants, no other standard form of income support is available; for long-term unemployed single people, net income thus comprises unemployment assistance. In each of the years 1980 to 1990, had a job offer been forthcoming at half the prevailing industrial wages, acceptance of that job would have exposed the job-taker both to income tax and to other direct deductions from gross income. Since in every year pay at half the prevailing industrial earnings lay above the thresholds for exemption from income tax and PRSI, both of these deductions at the full rate would have been levied on income. On accepting such a job offer, the unemployed single person would have been moving from an untaxed to a taxed environment.

This case is illustrated in table 24. Three points are worth noting about the transition from long-term unemployment to low-paid employment over this period. Firstly, the money value of unemployment assistance rose much more rapidly than gross earnings from employment between 1980 and 1990. Unemployment assistance for a single person more than tripled over the decade, rising from £17 a week in 1980 to £52 a week in 1990. The 1991 budget continued this trend, raising maximum unemployment assistance to £55 a week from late July 1991. Over the

Table 24

Benefits of employment at half average earnings to long-term unemployed single person

Year	Unemployment assistance (£/week)	Gross earnings in employment* (£/week)	Income tax (£/week)	PRSI levies (£/week)	Total tax (£/week)	After-tax income (£/week)	UA as percentage of after-tax income from work
1980	17.00	48.10	4.74	2.16	6.90	41.20	41.3
1981	20.40	56.13	6.18	2.67	8.85	47.28	43.1
1982	26.25	63.35	4.48	4.75	9.23	54.12	48.5
1983	28.90	70.78	7.13	6.02	13.15	57.63	50.1
1984	32.80	79.40	9.71	6.75	16.46	62.94	52.1
1985	34.95	85.73	11.25	7.29	18.54	67.19	52.0
1986	36.70	92.12	12.14	6.91	19.05	73.07	50.2
1987	37.80	96.82	13.79	7.50	21.29	75.53	50.0
1988	42.00	101.41	14.39	7.86	22.25	79.16	53.1
1989	47.00	105.49	14.46	8.18	22.63	82.86	56.7
1990†	52.00	108.68	14.51	8.42	22.93	85.75	60.6

*It is assumed that on gaining employment the previously unemployed single person earns half the prevailing level of average industrial earnings in manufacturing.
† in June 1990.
Sources: Tables 5, 12, 18.

same period, low pay (i.e. half average earnings) rose just two-and-a-quarter times, from £48.10 a week in 1980 to £108.68 a week in June 1990. Moreover, the pace of pay growth has decelerated sharply in the recent past.

Secondly, on moving to employment a person confronts effective direct tax rates that, even on half average pay, are very high, given the low levels of purchasing power involved. Even on low pay the effective personal tax rate on gross income (income tax together with PRSI and other income levies) rose from 14.4 per cent of gross income in 1980/81 to a peak of 22.0 per cent in 1987/88. Nor have the recent cuts in income tax provided much relief: by 1990/91 the effective tax rate still remained as high as 21.1 per cent of gross income. The principal causes of these high direct tax rates on low incomes lie in the fact that the same gross income was subject to three, and on occasion four, different income taxes. In the mid-1980s, in addition to income tax proper, gross income was subjected to deductions for PRSI, the 1 per cent youth employment levy, and the 1 per cent income levy. In one year—1982/83—the low-paid lost more in PRSI and income levies than they paid in income tax itself. In recent years, more than a third of the personal taxes taken from the low-paid have consisted of direct taxes other than income tax.

Thirdly, on taking jobs paying half the industrial wage, single people confronted extremely high marginal tax rate if they sought to improve their positions by earning more income. Over the decade as a whole the effective marginal tax rates on additional earnings rose from 29.5 per cent in 1980/81 to 37.75 per cent in 1990/91. Nor was their position significantly improved by the 1991 budget, which saw such marginal effective tax rates decline by only one percentage point, to 36.75 per cent.

Returning to work at low wages has thus become less attractive financially for single people among the long-term unemployed over the past decade. Whereas in 1980 unemployment assistance replaced just two-fifths of net income from low-paid employment, by 1990 three-fifths of potential net income from employment was provided through unemployment assistance.

The position of a married couple where one spouse moves from long-term unemployment to a job paying half the prevailing industrial wages is more difficult to assess, since it is here that the income tax and social welfare systems overlap to the greatest extent. In attempting to disentangle their complex interactions, five points are worth noting.

Tax alleviation for low-paid married couple with two dependent children

Year	Income exempt from income tax below: (£/week)	Ceiling income for medical card (£/week)	Family income supplement payable below income of (£/week):
1980/81	65.38	57.19	—
1981/82	76.92	67.73	—
1982/83	84.62	83.77	—
1983/84	92.31	94.35	—
1984/85	96.15	104.37	110.00
1985/86	101.92	110.88	118.00
1986/87	101.92	116.90	120.00
1987/88	101.92	120.92	126.00
1988/89	105.77	124.94	131.00
1989/90	123.08	127.94	136.00
1990/91	136.54	133.44	143.00

Sources: Revenue Commissioners; Department of Social Welfare.

Firstly, returning to work at half average industrial earnings would not have left the working spouse liable to income tax in any of the years 1980 to 1990; in all cases, earned income was within the general income tax exemption limit for married couples. The weekly incomes that married couples can earn without becoming liable to income tax are shown in table 25 for the years 1980 to 1990.

Secondly, while incomes were exempt from income tax proper in all cases, they were not exempt from other taxes on income. Re-employed spouses found themselves liable to PRSI from the first pound of income earned. However, some relief from PRSI was available: where earned income falls below the ceiling for holding a medical card, a part of the PRSI and income levy burden is transferred from the employee to the employer. The income ceilings below which a married couple with two children can retain a medical card are shown in table 25. Where actual earnings fall below this ceiling, the employee's health contributions and 1 per cent employment and training levy are paid for by the employer; as a result, in 1990/91 low-paid employees, where they were class A contributors, faced deductions of

PRSI and other levies at a rate of 5.5 per cent, compared with the 7.75 per cent charged on the incomes of higher earners. This concession has the paradoxical side-effect of *raising* the rate of payroll tax paid by employers where low-income workers are hired.

Thirdly, the introduction of the family income supplement in September 1984 has acted to top up the net incomes of low-paid married workers with children. The unemployed, single or married, cannot claim this supplement: it is available only to those households where one spouse is working a minimum of twenty hours a week and where incomes fall below the ceilings shown in table 25. In essence, the family income supplement boosts the net income of low-paid households, the amount of the supplement being determined by the scale of earnings and the number of children in the household. However, this supplementary benefit has suffered throughout its life from a low take-up rate: in 1989 only 6,066 families availed of it. Notwithstanding this, the scheme was further improved in the 1991 budget. The income ceiling for claimants was raised to £160 a week, and the actual payments are calculated at 60 per cent of the difference between that ceiling and actual earnings. In addition, a minimum weekly payment of £5 was introduced in 1991 for qualifying households.

Fourthly, an attempt was made in the 1990 budget to alleviate the PRSI burden on the very low-paid with the introduction of a PRSI exemption limit. However, the limit was pitched so low—at £60 a week, or just over a quarter of average industrial earnings—that the number of potential beneficiaries was very small. No attempt was made to raise this exemption limit in the 1991 budget.

Fifthly, a more determined effort to relieve the income tax burden on low-income households with children has been in evidence since 1989. In that year's budget the general income tax exemption limit was raised from £5,500 to £6,000 for a married couple. However, in a departure from the practice of previous years the Government also introduced an additional exemption allowance of £200 for each of the household's first four children. As a result, in 1989/90 a married couple with two children could earn up to £6,400 while remaining exempt from income tax. These exemption limits were raised further in the two succeeding budgets; for a married couple with two children, the income tax exemption limit was raised to £7,100 for 1990/91 and to £7,400 for 1991/92.

Table 26

Comparative tax and social welfare positions of married couple with two children, one spouse moving from long-term unemployment to low-paid job

Year	Unemployment assistance (£/week)	Gross earnings in employment* (£/week)	Tax and PRSI levies (£/week)	After-tax income (£/week)	UA as percentage of after-tax income	FIS†	UA as percentage of total income
1980	39.85	48.10	1.68	46.42	85.8	–	85.8
1981	46.70	56.13	2.10	54.03	86.4	–	86.4
1982	59.10	63.35	3.48	59.87	98.7	–	98.7
1983	65.15	70.78	3.89	66.89	97.4	–	97.4
1984	73.90	79.40	4.37	75.03	98.5	7.65	89.4
1985	78.75	85.73	4.72	81.01	97.2	8.07	88.4
1986	81.75	92.12	5.07	87.05	93.9	9.29	84.9
1987	84.20	96.82	5.33	91.49	92.0	14.59	79.2
1988	90.40	101.41	5.58	95.83	94.3	14.80	81.7
1989	97.00	105.49	5.80	99.69	97.3	18.31	82.2
1990	105.00	108.68	5.98	102.70	102.2	20.59	85.2

*It is assumed that on gaining employment, the previously unemployed spouse is paid half the prevailing level of average industrial earnings in manufacturing industry.
†Family income supplement was introduced in September 1984 to raise the incomes of low-paid workers with child dependants. It is calculated as follows: (Upper income limit – actual earnings) x FIS benefit rate. The upper limits for each year since 1984 are shown in table 24.

The effects of each of these factors are summarised in table 26. This table attempts to encapsulate the effects of a married person moving back into a job following a prolonged spell of unemployment in each of the years 1980 to 1990, assuming that such an individual was paid half average industrial wages. Because income from employment is so low, in each year it was exempt from income tax. The family holds a medical card, and so health contributions and the employment and training levy (and the 1 per cent income levy in the relevant years) are paid by the employer. This reduces the effective rate of tax to 5.5 per cent in the most recent years.

Where family income supplement is excluded—and it is claimed in only a small minority of cases—there is little financial incentive for married people to leave the ranks of the long-term unemployed and to re-join the work force, even where jobs are on offer. From 1982 onwards unemployment assistance for a married couple with two children provided at least 92 per cent of the earned income available from a job paying half average earnings. By 1990 a genuine poverty trap existed: the household would have lost cash each week if one spouse had returned to work at half average pay. The introduction of family income supplement in 1984 did improve the potential after-tax incomes of low-paid married workers. Where the supplement was claimed (and it is a discretionary allowance) it led to a significant topping up of the net incomes of those households with children where earned income was low.

The positive income wedge provided by the family income supplement may not have provided a great incentive for married people to return to work, but at least it has eliminated the poverty trap that saw the long-term unemployed experiencing a drop in real income on regaining employment. As can be seen from table 26, where this supplement is included as part of the total income from employment the poverty trap of 1990 disappears. Unemployment assistance replaced 79.2 per cent of income from employment—including family income supplement—in 1987, rising to a replacement rate of 85.2 per cent in 1990.

But the problems for the long-term unemployed re-joining the work force do not stop at the point of re-entry. Nobody goes back to work with the objective of being paid low wages. On half the average industrial earnings, married people among the long-term unemployed initially face an effective tax rate of only 5.5 per cent on any additional cash earned; but as such people's incomes begin to increase, social welfare benefits are lost, and the effective personal tax rate starts to rise very sharply.

Two factors contribute to this outcome. Firstly, on the social welfare side, households suffer the loss of graduated untaxed benefits as income from employment rises. For the year 1990/91 family income supplement terminated when earned income reached £143 a week, while households with two dependent children lost their medical cards when income exceeded £133.44 a week.

Secondly, on the income tax side, a problem experienced by all taxpayers is confronted. The raising of tax exemption levels for married couples with children, combined with the very high starting rates of tax (see table 23), produce a situation where households face very high marginal rates of income tax once income exceeds the tax exemption thresholds. In a very real sense, the effect of the income tax reforms introduced since 1988 has been to push the problem of very high marginal tax rates farther up the income distribution. These very high marginal tax rates materialise first when income earners fall into the tax net. This can be illustrated by monitoring the changing tax circumstances confronting married people returning to employment at low pay but whose incomes subsequently begin to climb.

For the tax year 1990/91, illustrated in table 26, where married people restarted employment at half the average earnings then prevailing, initially they would only have paid PRSI at a reduced rate of 5.5 per cent. Thus on earnings of £108.68 a week the only deductions would have been £5.98 in PRSI contributions. Such households would then have been left with a net income of £102.70 from employment. However, while weekly earnings were below the £105 available from unemployment assistance, such households were also entitled to claim family income supplement once one spouse was working. The family income supplement provided the household with a further £20.59 a week in state income support, leaving total income from employment at £123.29 after deduction of PRSI contributions. At this level, total income from employment—comprising earnings and the state income subsidy—came to £18.29 more than the alternative of unemployment assistance. In employment, the household has also at this level of income retained its medical card.

However, even before such households entered the tax net proper, the implicit marginal tax rates they faced were very high. While every additional £1 earned yielded 94.5p in after-tax income, it also resulted in a loss of 60p in family income supplement entitlements. As a result, the net income gained by households from a £1 increase in earned income came to just 34.5p. While the revealed personal tax rate stood at 5.5 per cent, the total implicit direct tax rate amounted to 65.5 per cent of additional income earned—a rate well above the marginal tax rate charged on the highest incomes.

Worse was to come. Where households' weekly earned incomes had risen to £130 and a £5 weekly pay increase was secured, the marginal tax rate on that increment exceeded 100 per cent, even though such households still remained outside the income tax net proper. When income exceeded £133.44 a week, entitlement to medical cards was lost. Not only was this in itself a significant reverse to the household, but as a result the PRSI and levies charged on all gross income rose from 5.5 to 7.75 per cent. Thus of the £5 increase in gross pay secured, additional PRSI contributions swallowed £3.31. The gain of £5 a week in earnings also resulted in the loss of £3 in family income supplement. Thus for a £5 gain in gross earnings, households have lost a total of £6.31, equivalent to an implicit effective marginal tax rate of 126.2 per cent.

In the tax year 1990/91, married couples with two children entered the tax net when weekly earnings exceeded £136.54. From this income point onwards, extra earnings were subjected to explicit direct taxes at a rate of 37.75 per cent. In addition, for each extra £1 earned, households continued to lose 60p until the family income supplement limit of £143 a week was exceeded. Thus for households with an earned income of £140 a week the effective tax rate on marginal earnings stood at 97.75 per cent. Above £143 a week, entitlements to family income supplement ceased.

For the tax year 1990/91 the interaction of taxes and benefits can be summarised as follows. Married people re-joining the work force initially faced very low marginal rates of tax, because their incomes were too low to fall within the tax net. On re-entering low-paid employment, such households could also avail of substantial family income supplement payments, serving as a positive income wedge. At half average gross weekly earnings of £108.68, households' net income from employment would have amounted to £123.29. With unemployment assistance available to households of this type at £105 a week, going back to work made financial sense.

However, the combined effects of the income tax and social welfare codes ensured that marginal tax rates on such households were extremely high where income increased from its low initial base. A rise in weekly pay from half to two-thirds of average earnings—in cash terms an increase of £36.32 a week—would have produced an increase of just £4.47 a week in net household income. An increase in gross earnings from employment from £108.68 to £145 a week would have induced a rise in net weekly income from £123.29 to £127.76. On the incremental income earned, this represents an effective tax rate of almost 88 per cent. In the process, households would have lost their medical cards.

The 1991 budget brought about some improvements. Households consisting of a married couple with two children do not enter the tax net until earnings exceed £142.31 a week. Family income supplement can be claimed until income reaches £160 a week, and those now qualifying receive a minimum cash payment of £5 weekly. But the essential problem of very high taxes—implicit and explicit—on low incomes remains. In conjunction with the high replacement incomes available from untaxed unemployment assistance, the financial incentives provided to the long-term unemployed to seek out employment opportunities are weak, and should be strengthened.

Many of the difficulties outlined in this chapter arise because the income tax system and the social welfare system speak different languages; much could be gained from their integration. Because effective marginal tax rates on the low-paid are so high—a consequence of benefit losses as well as direct tax charges—the integration of the tax and social welfare systems could improve significantly the returns on work available to those moving from long-term unemployment to jobs.

SEARCHING FOR LOWER TAXES ABROAD

The poverty traps and tax obstacles that must be surmounted by the long-term unemployed as they seek to regain employment are formidable; but the long-term unemployed are not the only ones who find that the tax system works against them as they seek a decent return from work. The next most heavily disadvantaged group are single people, particularly those possessing significant marketable skills or a high degree of training.

As was seen in chapter 4, the tax problems facing single people derive from two sources. Firstly, the basic tax allowances and tax bands available to them are set at only half the levels enjoyed by married couples, irrespective of whether one or both partners are working. Secondly, the progressiveness of the tax code pushes single taxpayers upwards towards the top rate of income tax very quickly. The combination of these forces means that in 1991/92 single taxpayers claiming the basic PAYE and PRSI tax allowances face a marginal effective income tax rate of 55.75 per cent on any earnings above £9,886 a year, and a marginal tax rate of 59.75 per cent on income exceeding £12,986 annually. In other words, single people face marginal personal tax rates in excess of 55 per cent even when their incomes are below average industrial earnings, and marginal tax rates of almost 60 per cent when their incomes are slightly above the industrial average.

Many young single people are not prepared to shoulder a tax burden of this magnitude. In table 3 it was shown that between April 1981 and April 1990 net emigration exceeded 200,000 people. While many of these emigrants were forced out of the domestic labour market by the shortage of jobs at home, an increasing proportion were voluntary emigrants who went abroad in search of higher net incomes than were available in Ireland. In the final years of the 1980s almost one in five of those leaving third-level education found their first jobs abroad. Many of the brightest and the best left Ireland, because the net incomes available to them were too low—principally because the income taxes they faced were too high.

8

The Irish labour market is not hermetically sealed; its participants are not irrevocably locked into it. Where opportunities abroad are better, in the form of job availability, higher real levels of purchasing power, or better promotion prospects, people will move out of the Irish labour market. And those who enjoy the greatest labour market flexibility—young single people unburdened with family responsibilities and possessing portable qualifications—will move fastest. The ease with which they can move is determined by the regulatory environment in host countries and the extent of the language barriers. The common language and the free movement of labour between Ireland and Britain has in effect created a joint labour market between the two countries; as a result the Irish labour supply is influenced not simply by incomes, taxes and employment opportunities at home but by incomes, taxes and job prospects in Britain. The same argument holds, though with less force because of the language barriers, for the labour markets of other European Community countries, since access to them is also free. The regulation of labour flows into the United States, Australia and New Zealand puts these markets into a different category, though their attractiveness is enhanced by a broadly common culture and language.

It follows that in assessing the impact of taxes on the domestic labour supply, policy makers cannot afford simply to base their decisions on the absolute levels of personal taxes in Ireland but on the height of those tax rates relative to other labour markets to which Irish labour enjoys access. For if Irish taxes become too high relative to those obtaining in other labour markets, labour resources will shift to the areas of greater opportunity.

During the 1980s, as income tax rates were climbing to ever-higher levels, personal tax rates in the principal labour markets to which Irish people emigrate were being reduced sharply. The most dramatic cuts in income tax rates, and from an Irish viewpoint the most relevant, were effected in Britain in 1988. There the standard tax rate was reduced to 25 per cent, while the top (and only other) rate was reduced from 60 to 40 per cent. Combined with the then buoyant employment conditions in Britain, these factors played a part in the exodus of young people from Ireland in the late 1980s. While the recession in Britain dating from the second half of 1990 has diminished employment opportunities there, the significant gap in income tax rates between the two countries will ensure a steady flow of Irish talent to Britain while that tax gap persists.

8

The main features of the two income tax codes as they operated in 1991/92 are summarised in table 27. In this comparison, only income taxes proper are surveyed; social insurance contributions and other income levies are excluded in both cases, as is the burden of Britain's poll taxes.

Table 27

Income tax in Ireland and Britain, 1991/92

	Ireland (£)	Britain (stg £)
1. Personal income tax allowances:		
— Single person	2,100	3,295
— Married couple, one working	4,200	5,015
— Married couple, both working	4,200	6,590
— Combined PAYE, PRSI allowances*	1,086	0
2. Personal income tax rates:		
— Standard income tax rate	29 %	25 %
— Middle income tax rate	48 %	—
— Top rate of income tax	52 %	40 %
3. Standard income tax bands width:		
— Single person	6,700	23,700
— Married couple, one working	13,400	23,700
— Married couple, both working	13,400	47,400
4. Top tax rate reached after taxable income of:		
— Single person	9,800	23,700
— Married couple, one working	19,600	23,700
— Married couple, both working	19,600	47,400

* Irish PAYE tax allowances: £800; Irish PRSI tax allowances: £286 (available only to PAYE employees).
Sources: *Principal Features of 1991 Budget*, presented to Dáil Éireann 30 January 1991; British budget, presented to Parliament 19 March 1991.

In Ireland, personal tax allowances were increased by £50 a year for single people and by £100 annually for married couples in the 1991/92 tax year to £2,100 and £4,200, respectively. The PAYE and PRSI allowances remained unchanged, at £800 and £286, respectively, for qualifying employees. The standard income tax band was widened by £200 to £6,700 in the case of single taxpayers and by £400 to £13,400 for married taxpayers. The standard rate of income tax was cut by one percentage point to 29 per cent, as was the top tax rate to 52 per cent. The middle tax rate of 48 per cent remained unchanged. Despite this trimming of the personal tax burden, single people still remained liable to income tax at the top rate of 52 per cent once their taxable incomes exceeded £9,800.

In Britain the Rooker-Wise amendment requires that tax bands and tax allowances be indexed upwards to take account of inflation each year, unless the government of the day explicitly decides otherwise. As a result, in the British budget of March 1991 single people's basic tax allowances were raised by 9.7 per cent to stg£3,295. The married person's tax allowance was left unchanged, at stg£1,720. In consequence, married couples' basic tax allowances where one spouse only was at work came to stg£5,015 for 1991/92; where both spouses are working, however, each can claim an individual single person's tax allowance. Where both spouses work, the basic tax allowances available to a married couple thus amounted to stg£6,590 in 1991/92.

British income tax rates were not changed in the 1991 budget. Two income tax rates remained in force, a standard rate of 25 per cent and a top rate of 40 per cent. However, tax bands were broadened significantly. The width of the standard band was increased by stg£3,000, or 14.5 per cent, to stg£23,700 for a single person. Married couples when both were working could avail of two sets of such tax bands in computing their income tax liabilities. As a result, single taxpayers had to earn a taxable income in excess of stg£23,700 before becoming liable to tax at the top rate of 40 per cent. For married couples in Britain it was possible to earn as much as stg£47,400 while still paying tax at the 25 per cent rate.

British taxpayers thus have the advantage over their Irish counterparts in facing lower income tax rates, in having access to bigger basic tax allowances, and above all by enjoying much wider tax bands at the standard rate of income tax. Table 28 illustrates these advantages in the case of single people earning £20,000 a year (in the appropriate currency) in both Britain and Ireland. For the 1991/92 tax year, where Irish taxpayers could claim the PAYE and PRSI tax allowances, there is little appreciable difference in the level of basic allowances between the two countries. The principal difference arose because of the differing widths of the standard tax rate bands in the two countries.

Relative income tax burdens in Ireland and Britain, single person, 1990/91 and 1991/92

	Ireland (£)		Britain (stg £)	
	1991/92	1990/91	1991/92	1990/91
Gross income	20,000	20,000	20,000	20,000
Single tax allowance	2,100	2,050	3,295	3,005
PAYE and PRSI tax allowances*	1,086	1,086	0	0
Taxable income	16,814	16,864	16,705	16,995
Income tax bill:				
— at standard tax rate	1,943	1,950	4,176	4,249
— at middle tax rate	1,488	1,488	0	0
— at top tax rate	3,647	3,850	0	0
Total income tax bill	7,078	7,288	4,176	4,249
Effective income tax rate†	35.4%	36.4%	20.9%	21.2%
Disposable after-tax income	12,922	12,712	15,824	15,751

* It is assumed that single Irish taxpayers can claim both the PAYE and PRSI tax allowances.
† Income tax bill as a percentage of gross pre-tax income.
Note: Only income tax proper is estimated here. Other taxes, including social insurance contributions and poll taxes, are excluded.

In Britain, with the standard rate tax band broadened to stg£23,700 in 1991/92, single people earning gross annual income of stg£20,000 were liable to tax at the 25 per cent rate only. After deduction of the relevant basic tax allowance, the total income tax bills payable by such people amounted to stg£4,176. This represented an effective income tax rate of 20.9 per cent on gross income; as a result, single people earning stg£20,000 a year took home four-fifths of their gross pay.

The contrast with the Irish tax load is striking. For 1991/92, on gross incomes of £20,000 single Irish employees were taxed successively at the 29 per cent, 48 per cent and 52 per cent rates. Over £7,000 of their gross incomes was subjected to income tax at the top rate of 52 per cent. As a result of being propelled so rapidly through a compressed progressive tax system, single taxpayers with incomes of £20,000 stood to lose 35.4 per cent of their earnings to the exchequer, even before allowing for the further deduction of social insurance contributions and levies. Single people earning £20,000 a year faced an effective income tax rate that was fifteen percentage points higher than that confronting their British counterparts earning stg£20,000 a year. Moreover, the marginal income tax rate charged on additional earnings in Ireland reached 52 per cent, more than twice the marginal income tax rate of 25 per cent faced by British employees on any extra cash earned. Thus Irish taxpayers lost more than half of any increases in pay, whereas in Britain single taxpayers gave up just a quarter of any additional income they earned.

Table 29 compares the position of married couples in Ireland and Britain during 1991/92 where one partner was working and earning £30,000 annually (in the appropriate currency). In this instance the gap between the effective income tax rates in the two countries is narrower than in the case of single people. The explanation for this lies in the fact that Irish married couples enjoyed access to two sets of single tax allowances and tax bands, even where only one partner is at work. The effective income tax rate in Ireland, at 31.7 per cent in 1991/92, still trailed ten percentage points behind the effective income tax rate of 21.5 per cent charged in Britain on married couples in similar financial circumstances.

The gap between the effective income tax rates in the two countries widens to almost fifteen percentage points once again in the case of married couples where both worked and where each partner earned £20,000 (in the appropriate currency) in 1991/92. This case is illustrated in table 30. In this instance the British working couple can each claim a set of individual tax allowances as well as enjoying access to a separate set of single person's tax bands. The income tax rate never exceeds 25 per cent; as a result the effective income tax rate on all income earned by the household came to only 20.9 per cent. In Ireland the effective tax charge, at 35.4 per cent of gross income, is almost fifteen percentage points higher.

Table 29				

Relative income tax burdens in Ireland and Britain, married couple, one spouse working, 1990/91 and 1991/92

	Ireland (£)		Britain (stg £)	
	1991/92	1990/91	1991/92	1990/91
Gross household income	30,000	30,000	30,000	30,000
Married couple's allowance	4,200	4,100	5,015	4,725
PAYE, PRSI tax allowances*	1,086	1,086	0	0
Taxable income	24,714	24,814	24,985	25,275
Income tax bill:				
— at standard income tax rate	3,886	3,900	5,925	5,175
— at middle income tax rate	2,976	2,976	—	—
— at top income tax rate	2,659	2,975	514	1,830
Total income tax bill	9,521	9,851	6,439	7,005
Effective income tax rate[†]	31.7%	32.8%	21.5%	23.4%
Disposable after-tax income	20,479	20,149	23,561	22,995

* It is assumed that working spouses in Ireland can claim both the PAYE and PRSI tax allowances.[†] Income tax bill as a percentage of gross pre-tax income.

In all cases where incomes are relatively high the British tax environment is more advantageous. Nor are the differences in effective tax rates marginal: they are substantial. The British income tax system thus provides a strong financial incentive to Irish residents earning above-average incomes to emigrate when jobs are offered. Those most likely to leave are young single people, both because they have the flexibility to depart easily and because the consequential tax savings are so great.

In the sphere of indirect taxes the case for harmonising VAT rates and excise duties between Britain and Ireland has long been accepted, in principle if not in practice. In the absence of such harmonisation, market liberalisation within Europe will result in a diversion of trade from Ireland and across its borders. The results manifest themselves in depressed levels of domestic business and lower tax yields. In effect, business is exported abroad when domestic rates of indirect tax are set at excessively high levels. Although it has received considerably less attention, this argument applies with equal force to direct taxes. Where

Table 30

Relative income tax burdens in Ireland and Britain, married couple, both spouses working, 1990/91 and 1991/92

	Ireland (£)		Britain (stg £)	
	1991/92	1990/91	1991/92	1990/91
Total household income	40,000	40,000	40,000	40,000
Joint basic tax allowances	4,200	4,100	6,590	6,010
PAYE/PRSI tax allowances*	2,172	2,172	0	0
Household taxable income	33,628	33,728	33,410	33,990
Joint income tax bill:				
— at standard income tax rate	3,886	3,900	8,353	8,498
— at middle income tax rate	2,976	2,976	0	0
— at top income tax rate	7,295	7,700	0	0
Total income tax bill	14,157	14,576	8,353	8,498
Effective income tax rate†	35.4%	36.4%	20.9%	21.2%
Household disposable income	25,843	25,424	31,647	31,502

* It is assumed that both the Irish spouses can claim both the PAYE and PRSI tax allowances.
† Household income tax bill as a percentage of gross household income.

rates of personal income tax in Ireland greatly exceed those obtaining in other labour markets to which access is unhindered, the result will be a parallel outflow of people, and the loss of their skills and training to the national economy and of the future flows of income tax revenue they would have paid had they remained at home. In order to preserve and enhance the stock of human capital in the country, tax harmonisation is as vital in the income tax sphere as in the field of indirect taxation.

MAKING SENSE OF THE LABOUR MARKET

Taken as a whole, the 1980s were disappointing years for the Irish economy. No matter what measuring rod is applied, economic performance was poor. Economic growth remained low for most of the decade, reviving only from 1987 onwards. Nowhere was performance more disappointing than in the labour market. Between 1980 and 1990 total employment fell, unemployment doubled, and the country lost the equivalent of 6 per cent of its 1980 population through net emigration. The deterioration in domestic labour market conditions and the emigration this engendered was in part responsible for the fact that by the end of the decade the population was once more in decline.

In comparison with other industrial countries, Ireland's economic performance up to 1987 was miserable. Over the years 1979 to 1987, and measured against the twenty-four industrial countries comprising the OECD, Ireland ranked twenty-second on economic growth achieved, twenty-third on employment growth, and twenty-third on the height of unemployment. The decline in employment and the escalation of unemployment during these years was associated with a sharp and continuous rise both in the scale of public spending and the size of the personal tax burden. Without assigning any cause at this stage, it is sufficient to note that high levels of public spending, large public sector deficits and heavy tax burdens were associated with job destruction rather than job creation.

While annual inflation rates had been falling throughout the 1980s, it was not until 1987 that the real economy began to revive. Over the years 1987 to 1990 economic growth became particularly vibrant, and slowly—perhaps too slowly—this was reflected in an improvement in labour market conditions. In particular, employment began to expand once again. In the three years from April 1987 to April 1990 the number of people at work rose by 40,000 or 3.7 per cent. In the four years ending 1990, the Irish economy expanded by one-sixth in size when measured by the GNP growth. While the translation of economic growth into employment growth may not have been as high as

9

desired, at least employment was beginning to move in the right direction once again.

This period of economic regeneration and expansion in employment was associated with a sharp reduction both in current and capital spending by the state, a fall in public sector deficits, and the initiation of a programme of tax cuts for those at work.

In contrasting the economic experience of the 1980–86 period and its associated public spending and personal tax regime with that of the 1987–90 period, it must be accepted that the latter was marked by the emergence of particularly favourable international economic conditions. From 1987 growth in Ireland's near neighbours and trading partners was particularly strong, and some of the additional demand generated spilled over into the Irish economy. The period witnessed the revitalisation of the European economy and the encouragement of hopes that strong growth in the future would be fostered by the completion of the single European market.

Nevertheless, the turnaround in Ireland's economic fortunes was due to more than good luck; it was also due to good management. Moreover, the bouquets for that good management should be widely distributed. It is usual to ascribe responsibility for economic management, for good or ill, to the Government of the day. But these were not usual times. Through the 'Tallaght Strategy', Fine Gael provided opposition support for the minority Fianna Fáil Government of 1987–89; policy continuity since then has been provided by a coalition of Fianna Fáil and the Progressive Democrats. The Programme for National Recovery, 1988–90, negotiated by the social partners, delivered industrial peace and a moderate rate of growth in private sector pay.

While the strength of demand conditions abroad and the revival of demand at home played the principal part in improving labour market conditions in the final years of the decade, the impact of specific measures geared towards making the labour market work more effectively cannot be ignored, and should not be neglected. For although many find the description distasteful, the labour market is a market that functions like any other. The net returns to work, as measured by real after-tax spending power, do influence the numbers seeking work, particularly among marginal labour market participants. The net returns to work in Ireland relative to those in similar countries will exert an influence on the numbers of young people who will enter the labour market at home and on those who will

9

seek their initial employment abroad. The net returns from work relative to the net returns from not working will influence the disposition of people as between work and non-work. Thus the real purchasing power of earned income, and changes in that purchasing power over time, will determine whether people work, how they work, where they work. In short, real wages do influence the domestic supply of labour.

On the other side of the labour market, the number of employees an employer wishes to hire will be influenced by the cost of labour in its own right and its cost relative to other, substitutable factors of production. In short, the price of labour to employers will influence their demand for labour.

Real wages—the real price of labour—differ when viewed from the perspective of employees and employers, and for a number of reasons. First of all, the appropriate deflator that translates employees' net money incomes into real incomes is the consumer price index. This index measures not only trends in the underlying price of goods and services purchased by consumers but also the indirect taxes imposed on them by governments. In the case of employers, real income—from which real wages must be paid—is represented by cash income deflated by the output price index, which does not include indirect taxes. Thus the existence of indirect taxes in themselves drives an initial wedge between real wages as seen by employees and real income as seen by employers. This can lead to considerable dislocation in the labour market, where pay bargains link increases in money wages to increases in consumer prices. For where such increases in consumer prices are attributable to increases in indirect taxes, employers are not receiving sufficient increases in their own incomes with which to finance the agreed indexed increases in pay without eroding their own profit margins.

Secondly, and much more seriously, the distorting effects of the indirect tax wedge are greatly exacerbated by the direct tax wedge. On the one hand, high levels of personal tax on the incomes of employees create a large gap between what employers pay in gross wages and what employees receive in net income after tax. On the other hand, payroll taxes levied on the gross incomes of the employees hired by an employer and paid by the employer add further to the gap between what it costs the employer to hire employees and what employees receive in their pay-packets.

Direct taxes thus drive a wedge between the cost of labour and the returns from work. This disrupts the smooth working of the forces of supply and demand in the labour market, since it means that employers and employees are no longer talking the same language about wages. The wages offered by employers differ substantially from the wages received by employees, because of the tax wedge.

Viewed from the employee's side of the labour market, fewer workers will offer themselves for employment at the after-tax incomes they would receive than at the gross wages proffered by employers. Similarly, employers would hire more workers if they had to pay only the after-tax incomes actually received by employees rather than the gross payroll costs they must bear. The existence of a tax wedge induces both the supply and demand for labour to contract. Other things being equal, a large personal tax wedge works to reduce the level of employment, both by curbing the supply of labour and by restricting the demand for labour.

The distortions occasioned by the personal tax wedge in the labour market can be further accentuated by developments outside the labour market, principally in the sphere of social welfare. The evolution of an extensive social welfare safety net for the unemployed has widened the spectrum of choices confronting individuals. The alternatives do not consist of working and earning an income or not working and not earning an income; instead, they comprise the choice of working and earning an income that will be highly taxed, or not working and drawing a lower, but untaxed, social welfare income. In financial terms, the ultimate decision will be determined by the extent to which the income from non-work adequately replaces the after-tax income from work.

The tax wedge increased sharply and continuously for those on average earnings for much of the 1980s, driven upwards by rising effective tax rates on average employees' incomes and by increases in employers' social insurance contributions. Single employees being paid average industrial earnings in manufacturing saw their effective personal tax rates rise from 26.9 per cent of gross income in 1980/81 to a peak of 35.4 per cent in 1987/88. The tax wedge, measured in this instance by average employees' take-home pay as a proportion of the total labour cost to the employer, also increased in size over this period.

Single employees' take-home pay fell from 66.6 per cent of what it cost employers to hire them in 1980/81 to 57.5 per cent in 1987/88. As a result, the cost to the employer of granting the average single employee a £1 increase in net income rose from £1.82 in 1980/81 to £2.55 in 1987/88.

While starting from a lower base, the effective income tax rate borne by a married couple with two children where one spouse was working and being paid average industrial earnings rose even more rapidly. In 1980/81 such a household suffered an effective personal tax rate of 14.4 per cent of gross income. By 1988/89 the effective tax rate levied on gross income had risen to 25.5 per cent. Again, the tax wedge widened in this case. As a proportion of the cost to the employer, the married spouse on average earnings took home 78.0 per cent in 1980/81; by 1988/89 this proportion had declined to 66.2 per cent.

The proportion of average earnings replaced by unemployment benefits exhibited two quite different trends during the 1980s, depending on the duration of unemployment. Those on short-term unemployment benefits suffered a sharp decline in the amount of previous income replaced by the combination of unemployment benefit and pay-related benefit. For those who had previously received average industrial earnings, the income replacement ratio fell from 61.3 per cent in 1980 to 43.1 per cent in 1990 if single, and from 82.9 to 71.1 per cent if married with two children. This decline resulted from the restrictions on the proportion of previous earned income that could be claimed as benefit, and from the very sharp induced erosion of pay-related benefit.

In contrast, for the long-term unemployed the proportion of prospective average incomes provided by unemployment assistance rose continuously throughout the decade, both for single and married claimants. In the case of single people, income replacement rose from 24.2 per cent of average after-tax earnings in 1980/81 to 35.2 per cent in 1990/91. The long-term income replacement ratio for married couples with two children rose from 47.2 per cent of average after-tax earnings in 1980/81 to 63.6 per cent in 1990/91.

From the 1988 budget onwards, significant innovations were introduced that helped to ameliorate the effects of a rapidly deteriorating tax and transfer system. The broad thrust of the changes can be summarised thus. Firstly, there were significant increases in the breadth of the tax bands. Secondly, tax rates were reduced, the highest falling from 58 to 52 per cent, the lowest (standard) rate being cut from 35 to 29 per cent with the introduction of the 1991 budget. Thirdly, an attempt was made to improve the working environment for the low-paid, principally through the raising of tax exemption limits, particularly for families with children, and also by the introduction of a PRSI exemption limit where earnings fall below £60 a week. Fourthly, family income supplement was strengthened, improving the incentives to households with children to seek work, even at low pay.

As a result of these changes, effective tax rates have declined somewhat for those on average earnings, whether married or single, and the size of the tax wedge has contracted also. The increase in unemployment benefits in 1990/91 led to an increase in the proportion of average earnings replaced by such benefits, both for the short-term and long-term unemployed.

The changes introduced in the very recent past are welcome, both because they go some small way to improving the operation of the labour market mechanism itself and because they indicate a greater realisation of the detrimental effects on employment created by high taxes. However, even when account is taken of these changes, personal tax burdens remain much heavier and tax wedges much wider than they were a decade ago. The foundations that have been laid need to be built upon.

In constructing further packages of tax reforms, three areas need to be addressed if the labour market is to function more smoothly. Firstly, both average and marginal tax rates remain very high at average income levels. Because they enjoy only half the tax allowances and tax bands of their married counter-parts, single taxpayers are treated particularly harshly by the existing tax regime. Tax rates are both too high and rise too steeply at relatively low income levels. The starting rate of 29 per cent in 1991/92 is exceptionally high by international standards. The Irish tax code also possesses the remarkable characteristic of being highly progressive at relatively low levels of income but regressive at high levels of income. Because of the ceilings on income on which employees' PRSI is chargeable, effective tax rates *fall* when earned income is high. As a result, the effective tax rate borne by a single person earning average industrial pay still stood at 32.1 per cent in 1990/91; in other words, single people with average earnings lost one-third of their gross incomes through direct taxes. Moreover, because of the progressiveness of the tax code, such people faced effective marginal tax rates of 55.75 per cent on any additional income earned. In this instance, marginal tax rates remain close to the peak levels attained during the 1980s; there has been no relief.

This type of tax structure has two adverse effects on the labour market. Firstly, faced with this tax code, young single people armed with high educational qualifications and therefore high earning potential may simply decide not to participate in the Irish labour market: they may instead move abroad in search of a more accommodating tax regime. Secondly, given the progressiveness of the tax code, single people in employment may not feel it worth while acquiring additional skills. In both cases the skills base of the economy is eroded and the potential for future growth diminished. The extensive flow of young graduates abroad in recent years suggests that this line of reasoning is no hypothetical construct: young people are voting against the Irish tax system by leaving it.

The second important area requiring reform is the position of the low-paid. Even at half the level of average earnings, a single person bears an effective income tax rate of 21.1 per cent of gross income, and faces a marginal tax rate of 36.75 per cent in 1991/92 on any additional pay earned. Because of the size of the tax bite, a single person on unemployment assistance enjoys three-fifths of the net income of a person at work earning half the average level of industrial pay.

The position of an unemployed married couple with two children where one spouse is contemplating a return to employment is more difficult to assess, because of the interaction of the tax and benefit systems. Where one spouse returns to work at half average industrial earnings, no income tax is charged; but social insurance contributions and income levies are payable, though at reduced rates, on every penny earned. In such circumstances the disposable income of the household would *fall* if one spouse returned to work at half industrial earnings. If full family income supplement is claimed, a return to work makes financial sense, though the increase in net household income is small. The exemption from PRSI for the low-paid introduced in the 1990 budget is of no use to such a household, since it applies only to those earning less than £60 a week.

The marginal tax rates facing such a household if earnings increase are immense. They enter the tax code, bearing income tax for the first time; as income increases they are required to pay the health contribution and the employment and training levy; they receive reduced rates of family income supplement; and they eventually lose entitlement to their medical card.

This introduces the third area that requires reform: the administration of the tax and social welfare systems. There is an urgent need, if not to integrate the income tax and social insurance contribution systems, at least to make them run parallel to each other. The existing position, where levels of exemption and incidence vary so widely, creates too many distortions. Again, the tax and social welfare systems, which operate independently at present, are too often to be found pulling in different directions. The result is a Byzantine system, hard to understand, difficult to administer, and of uncertain effect.

THE WAY AHEAD

Politicians of all persuasions have been more sophisticated in their attitudes to budgetary policy in general, and to taxation in particular, in recent years. For a start, the perception of direct taxes as a form of punishment inflicted by the Government on those who have the temerity to earn high incomes has all but disappeared. The top rate of income tax, which reached 77 per cent in the mid-1970s, was twenty-five percentage points lower, at 52 per cent, in the fiscal year 1991/92. Nor is any political party committed to returning income tax rates to such high levels on ideological grounds; as a political pastime, 'soaking the rich' has become unfashionable.

The second significant advance has been the acceptance of a link between the level of public spending and the weight of the tax burden. With recourse to large-scale public borrowing no longer contemplated by any political party, the relationship between spending and taxing has become transparent. Politicians can no longer take refuge, as they did during the 1970s and early 1980s, in the subterfuge that increased provision of public services can be financed continuously by raising public borrowing rather than by raising taxes.

The acceptance of the link between spending and tax has caused a significant shift in political perspectives on taxation itself: it has stopped the public spending tail wagging the taxing dog. Through much of the 1970s and into the 1980s, prior increases in public spending were the engines that caused taxes to rise subsequently. During that era, Governments first decided their desired levels of public spending and then set taxes at whatever levels were necessary to finance that expenditure while at the same time maintaining a veneer of respectability on the quantum of public borrowing.

10

This whole economic world-view was reversed from 1987 onwards. Expenditure was pruned back both to contain the level of public borrowing and to clear the way for subsequent tax cuts. At last, the public's unwillingness to pay more taxes began to curb the Government's desire to spend.

The third breakthrough occurred in a related area. There was a growing realisation among politicians of all colorations that the imposition of higher taxes caused individuals to alter their economic behaviour. Where taxation policy in the past was seen as a passive, residual element in the economic equation, its capacity to stimulate and promote economic growth has now been recognised more clearly. This has created the opportunity to use tax cuts as an active and positive instrument of economic policy that can be harnessed to generate economic expansion in the future.

Learning these lessons has proved expensive, as the weight of the personal tax burden and the size of the national debt both testify. To ensure that even a modicum of value is salvaged for the public money already spent, it is imperative that these lessons be pressed into service in the future: the recognition of problems is not synonymous with their solution. Despite the strength of the economic recovery in the four years ending 1990 and the continuance of growth at a slower level into 1991, three major problems continue to blight economic performance. Nor can the effects of these fundamental problems be contained within the economic sphere: for pervasive unemployment, persistent high emigration and the extensiveness of low-paid employment all shape the nature of Irish society today.

Despite the years of boom and bloom, almost one in every five members of the labour force remains unemployed. By March 1991 the numbers registered as unemployed had risen to 246,515, representing 18.9 per cent of the labour force. This surge in unemployment, which continued throughout the 1980s and into the 1990s, has occurred despite persistent net emigration over the past decade, which between April 1981 and April 1990 exceeded 200,000. The termination of net emigration in the year to April 1991 has resulted in a further sharp upward shift in the level of unemployment.

Of those at work, many earn low pay, where pay is defined as real after-tax purchasing power. At the bottom of the labour market, the problems of those on low pay are compounded by the fact that effective tax rates on work, both average and marginal, are very high when after-tax income from employment is compared with substitute or replacement incomes available from social welfare.

Clearly, the scale of these problems is so great, individually and collectively, that they cannot be solved at a stroke. However, they must be addressed in a systematic way over time if any

10

progress is to be made towards their alleviation. A restructuring of the income tax and social welfare systems would be the first tentative step on the road to a solution. A key element in any long-term approach must be the integration of the social welfare and income tax codes. Many of the difficulties that arise at present occur because these two systems operate independently and do not speak the same language. Integrating them, and financing all social insurance benefits from central Government funds, would make the labour market operate more efficiently and more effectively.

The first innovation should be effected on the income tax side. The many forms of income tax now collected—income tax proper, health and social insurance contributions, the 1 per cent training levy—need to be consolidated into a single set of income tax rates and accompanied by a single schedule of income tax thresholds, tax allowances, and tax bands. At once this would make transparent the actual rates of direct tax that are charged on income; such transparency, by revealing the real height of income taxes, would concentrate the minds of politicians on reducing them. At the same time, providing for a single schedule of tax thresholds, tax allowances and tax bands would eliminate the more glaring poverty traps at present encountered by those in employment.

Initially, the biggest gain would be recorded by the low-paid. At present, unless they earn less than £60 a week, members of this group find themselves liable to income taxes at up to 7.75 per cent on all income earned, even though they may be officially exempt from the income tax net itself! With an integrated and streamlined single income tax system they would not become liable to any direct taxes on their income until they had exhausted their income tax allowances or passed the income tax exemption threshold.

Furthermore, there could be significant incidental gains to the exchequer that would hold down the rates at which any integrated income tax were levied. With the abolition of earmarked social insurance contributions for earmarked benefits and their replacement with an integrated tax financing general Government expenditure, the existing case for reduced rates of social insurance contributions in the public service would collapse. This would represent a worthwhile gain in equity.

More broadly, an integrated income tax and social welfare system would allow income from both employment and social welfare benefits to be assessable for direct taxation on an equal footing. It would not matter whether income was earned or derived from social welfare: if there were enough of it, it would be taxed. Moreover, where a household enjoyed income from both of these sources in the course of a year, such incomes would be aggregated for direct taxation purposes.

To further strengthen the position of those in low-paid employment, payments under the innovative family income supplement scheme could be exempted from income tax. This supplement is paid to low-income households with children on a sliding scale until the earnings ceiling is reached; for the tax year 1991/92 that ceiling is £160 a week.

Those who would gain unambiguously from this first stage of integration would be workers in low-paid employment; most other taxpayers and benefit recipients would remain relatively unaffected. Even where income from social welfare benefits became assessable for income tax, few recipients would become liable for actual tax payments, for the great majority would find that their social welfare incomes were so small as to exempt them from direct taxation.

In the fiscal year 1991/92 unemployment assistance for a single person was raised to £55 a week. However, for that year single people earning less than £65 a week were exempt from income tax. Thus, even if such a single person's unemployment assistance payments were redefined as income they would not become liable to income tax. Similarly, for 1991/92 a household of two adults and two children required an income in excess of £7,400 annually before income tax became payable. The potential losers in this first phase might include those who in the course of a year enjoyed a joint income from employment and social welfare benefits, as well as those who are at present paying reduced rates of social insurance contribution.

Initially with tax integration the revealed rate of income tax would rise, perhaps to 35 per cent from its 29 per cent level in 1991/92. The second stage of integration would thus focus on reducing this rate of tax and the weight of the personal tax burden generally. Three separate initiatives, all of them costly, are needed to secure these results.

Firstly, basic tax allowances for single and married people should be raised initially to the general tax exemption limits now obtaining, and then indexed to inflation thereafter. The present position is anomalous in the extreme. For 1991/92, single people earning less than £3,400 annually were exempt from income tax altogether. Yet if their annual incomes were increased to £4,000 they were only permitted to claim a basic allowance of £2,100. The remainder of their incomes was liable to income tax if no further tax allowances could be claimed. Similarly, married couples with no children were exempt from tax in 1991/92 if their joint incomes fell below £6,800: however, if such households were earning a joint income of, say, £8,000 their basic tax allowance amounted to just £4,200 and potentially they were liable to income tax on the remainder. By raising basic tax allowances to the level of existing tax exemption thresholds the tax load would be lightened for all taxpayers. To ease the cost of transition, the existing PAYE and PRSI tax allowances of £800 and £286, respectively, could be abolished in the process.

Secondly, the existing tax code is heavily biased against single people, as married couples enjoy twice the single person's tax allowances and tax bands whether one or both spouses are working. Very high effective rates of income tax on the earnings of single people provide them with a strong financial incentive to emigrate; this incentive becomes even more powerful where such people are highly trained and where they possess internationally marketable skills. To block this 'brain drain', once tax allowances have been raised to the existing income tax exemption thresholds, further real increases in tax allowances should be granted in the form of *earned* income allowances. They would thus be available only to those at work, whether married or single.

Thirdly, and most importantly, the initial integrated tax rate of around 35 per cent would be excessively high. Already, at 29 per cent in 1991/92, Ireland's initial rate of income tax is the second-highest of all western industrial countries. It would thus be necessary to interpose a new low rate of income tax, perhaps at around 15 per cent, before the new standard tax rate of 35 per cent was reached.

An integrated and staged reform programme of this type could harness much of the potential that is wasted today. It would improve the incentive to work, benefit the low-paid especially, and blunt the incentive to emigrate, while lightening the personal tax burden for all taxpayers. Its first stage would be virtually costless; its second stage would inevitably involve considerable expense to the exchequer in the form of forgone tax revenues.

The high cost of such a programme is not in itself a sufficient reason to stall on the introduction of a tax reform package.

The costs could be met by a progressive scaling down of the levels of current public spending. Indeed, it should be made clear from the outset that this is the only road along which a tax reform package can be carried. Nor should such reductions in public spending levels be a cause of anxiety: economic growth in Ireland was never lower than when public spending was rising very rapidly during the first half of the 1980s, and was rarely higher than in the 1987–90 period, when the Government was cutting back severely on its own expenditure.